John Watson Alvord

Fifth semi-annual report on schools for freedmen

January 1, 1868

John Watson Alvord

Fifth semi-annual report on schools for freedmen
January 1, 1868

ISBN/EAN: 9783337278526

Printed in Europe, USA, Canada, Australia, Japan

Cover: Foto ©Paul-Georg Meister /pixelio.de

More available books at **www.hansebooks.com**

FIFTH SEMI-ANNUAL REPORT

ON

SCHOOLS FOR FREEDMEN,

JANUARY 1, 1868,

BY

J. W. ALVORD,

GEN. SUPT. SCHOOLS, BUREAU REFUGEES, FREEDMEN AND ABANDONED LANDS.

WASHINGTON:
GOVERNMENT PRINTING OFFICE.
1868.

FIFTH SEMI-ANNUAL REPORT

ON

SCHOOLS FOR FREEDMEN.

War Department, Bureau of Refugees, Freedmen, &c.,
Office General Superintendent of Schools,
Washington, D. C., January 1, 1868.

General : I have the honor to submit my fifth semi-annual report of schools under the superintendence of this bureau for the six months ending December 31, 1867.

A full understanding of this educational work requires a brief historical survey of the field now occupied, with some knowledge of that previous period in which it was initiated.

The rebellion in its first stages awakened a belief among the slaves that by means of it they were to escape from bondage. The "northern army coming," as they heard, was to them the assured harbinger of liberty. Aspirations, deep and strong, were at once awakened in anticipation of privileges which this freedom was to bring them, and they evinced an instinctive *preparation* for these privileges.

As yet there had been no proclamation of emancipation. The local orders to that effect, by Generals Frémont and Hunter, were soon revoked. Panic-stricken fugitives all along the lines were returned, but the hopes of these poor people were irrepressible. They felt assured that deliverance had come.

When our armies entered the south and the facts there were brought to light, two important things appeared : first, a surprising thirst for knowledge among the negroes ; second, teachers in large numbers volunteering to instruct them. Hence, as soon as access could be obtained, schools among the colored people were successfully established. Many, indeed, scoffed ; more doubted ; but it is a remarkable fact that the earliest efforts to impart knowledge to these darkened minds found them fully prepared for its reception.

A correlative preparation of *instructors* deserves notice. Many ardent persons had long waited for the work, purposing to volunteer in it as soon as opportunity offered. A still larger number were stirred in heart by the recent report of tens of thousands of freedmen now accessible. Thus teachers of culture and the best possible moral preparation were ready from the first. A ripe, inviting harvest was met by prompt and willing reapers.

First efforts.—The army, to some extent, had carried its own instructors. Negro servants of officers studied at the camp-fires of fellow-servants. Laborers learned of comrades. On the enlistment of colored troops chaplains became instructors, and, with other officers detailed for this service, taught, in some regiments, the whole rank and file. In the campaigns of 1864 and 1865, the Christian Commission had 50 teachers employed during a large portion of their time in colored camps and regiments.

It is supposed that at the close of the war 20,000 colored soldiers could read intelligently, and a much larger number were in the elements of learning.

It should be said that schools for *free colored persons*, under various restrictions, had for years existed in the larger cities of the southern States ; slaves, however, in city or country could only learn by stealth, and in most of the States high penalties existed for teaching them.

The American Missionary Association, whose labors from the first had been given to the African race in this and other countries, founded a school for pupils irrespective of color at Berea, Kentucky, previous to the rebellion. It was interrupted only while the war lasted.

First schools for "contrabands."—The earliest school at the south for freedmen, or "contrabands," as they were then called, was commenced by the above association at Fortress Monroe, September 17, 1861. During the day it was for children, and at night for adults.

Soon after the capture of Port Royal, Rev. Solomon Peck, D. D., of Boston, went, with a military permit, to Beaufort, South Carolina, and established a day school, which in a few weeks numbered 60 pupils, ranging in age from six to 15 years. This school was commenced on the 8th of January, 1862.

Barnard K. Lee, jr., one of the superintendents of "contrabands," assisted by other government officers, opened a Sabbath and day school at Hilton Head, South Carolina, the latter part of January.

Another school in Beaufort, opened February 1, 1862, was taught for a short time by an agent of the American Missionary Association in what was called the " Praise House."

Edward L. Pierce, esq., of Boston, who had early in January been sent out by the Secretary of the Treasury to examine the condition of the abandoned plantations on the Sea islands, and the labor of the colored people upon them, aided by his presence in these first efforts. He had also, with the assistance of Reverends E. E. Hale and J. M. Manning, of Boston, secured the services of three teachers, who went about the middle of February, and opened schools on Hilton Head island.

Formation of educational societies.—A more general movement was soon inaugurated. Mr. Pierce's interesting report to Mr. Chase had produced a strong impression, and the Rev. Mansfield French, on the 2d of January, 1862, was deputed by the government to "examine the condition of the negroes along the whole southern coast." On his return in February, General W. T. Sherman and Commodore DuPont united by letters in an appeal to the benevolent of the north in behalf of the destitute within the limits of their command.

Public meetings were at once held in Boston, New York, and Philadelphia. The reports of Messrs. Pierce and French, *recommending " the establishment of schools* and sending supplies to the destitute," were promptly acted upon in the former city by the formation of the " Boston Educational Commission," February 7, and in New York by the "Freedmen's Relief Association," instituted February 20, and on the 3d of March, 1862, 52 teachers, missionaries, and superintendents (40 men and 12 women) sailed from New York for Port Royal. These persons were sent in charge of the Treasury agent, but under the special patronage of the Freedmen's Relief Association; a large portion of them, however, (25 men and 4 women,) were selected and commissioned by the Boston society. The whole company had transportation and subsistence furnished by the government, which also, after a short time, paid the salaries of the superintendents. They were at first employed mainly in the organization of labor and the relief of physical want; but schools were immediately commenced by teachers at various points on the Sea islands.

Work reported to Secretary of Treasury.—Other teachers followed in quick succession, and the whole enterprise, as reported in June following to the Secretary of the Treasury, showed 86 persons in the field—a society in Philadelphia, called the "Port Royal Relief Commission," organized March 3, 1862, having contributed funds, provisions, and a number of laborers.

On the 28th of June this work was transferred to the War Department, under the local charge of Brig. Gen. Rufus Saxton, then military governor of South Carolina.

First schools at the national capital.—At the capital there had been some earlier efforts. A school for "contrabands" was begun in Washington in the latter part of the summer of 1861, by Rev. D. L. Johnson. This was a night school and numbered 25 pupils. Soon after a day school was opened of about the same number. In April, 1862, a school was commenced by the American Tract Society of New York, in "Duff Green Row," then crowded with "contrabands," imprisoned as captured material of war. In May, 1862, the American Missionary Association started their first mission in Washington. It engaged in Christian work and elementary teaching.

Educational societies at the west—Miscellaneous efforts.—Educational societies were also formed in Cincinnati and Chicago. The former, in the spring of 1863, sent teachers to the camps of colored troops on the Mississippi, and the latter commenced its operations in the autumn following. Several religious denominations sent teachers to various points. Individuals sought the field and worked alone. In short, there was soon a general waking up of philanthropic hearts and volunteering of men and women in an effective, though of necessity disjointed, beginning of this great work. Wherever our troops broke through the lines of the enemy schools followed. At Hampton, Beaufort, North Carolina, Roanoke Island, and New Orleans, they were soon in operation. A very efficient system was instituted for Louisiana, in the early part of 1864, by Major General N. P. Banks, then in command of that State. It was supported by a military tax upon the whole population.

Schools in Savannah.—Schools were opened in Savannah, Georgia, on the entrance of General Sherman, in December, 1864, and 500 pupils were at once enrolled. Ten intelligent colored persons were the first teachers, and nearly $1,000 were immediately contributed by the negroes for their support. This work was organized by the secretary of the American Tract Society, Boston. Two of the largest of these schools were in "Bryan's slave mart," whose platforms, occupied a few days before by bondmen for the auction, became crowded with children of the same class learning to read.

Whole southern country opened.—When the war ended the whole southern country was at once opened and 4,000,000 of emancipated slaves were upon our hands; degraded and ignorant indeed, yet, with scarcely an exception, confiding in their northern friends, grateful for what had been done for them, and earnestly asking for continued instruction.

There was work enough, and it had been worthily commenced, but there was need of organization, protection from threatened violence, and means to prosecute the undertaking on a much larger scale.

Freedmen's Bureau instituted.—This bureau was created by act of Congress March 3, 1865, and, at the call of the President, Maj. Gen. O. O. Howard hastened from the right wing of the army of General Sherman as its Commissioner.

Work to be done.—An immense and novel work was upon his hands. It had no precedents. Emancipation, forced upon unwilling masters, among whom the emancipated in utter dependence were still obliged to dwell, made a case wholly anomalous. Physical want, medical aid to the sick, asylums for the infirm and orphans, regulation of labor, administration of justice, care of abandoned lands, as well as educational facilities for such large numbers, imposed a task not only momentous, but embarrassing.

Work not to be taken from voluntary patrons.—The first determination of the Commissioner was not to take this great charity from the hands of its voluntary patrons. The people of the north had been pouring out supplies for suffering soldiers, and this general flow of philanthropy was not to subside. It turned naturally to the freedmen. To lift them up, especially by education, was legitimately the work of the people. And yet there was need of cutting broader channels for the strong current of such noble endeavors. By unity, the forces employed could be economized, and the sphere of effort enlarged, dignified, and made permanent by well defined and vigorous government support.

Circular No. 2.—The Commissioner, therefore, said in his Circular No. 2, May 19, 1865:

The educational and moral condition of the people will not be forgotten. The utmost facility will be offered to benevolent and religious organizations and State authorities in the maintenance of good schools for refugees and freedmen until a system of free schools can be suported by the reorganized local governments. * * * It is not my purpose to supersede the benevolent agencies already engaged in the work of education, but to systematize and facilitate them.

Credit due benevolent associations.—In his first report the Commissioner gave great credit to these agencies : " Really wonderful results had been accomplished through the disinterested efforts of benevolent associations working in connection with the government." But arrangements were soon made to give, on a larger scale, systematic and impartial aid to all of them. This consisted in turning over for school use temporary government buildings no longer needed for military purposes, and buildings seized from disloyal owners ; also transportation for teachers, books, and school furniture, with quarters and rations for teachers and superintendents when on duty.

Use of refugees' and freedmen's fund.—Schools were taken in charge by the bureau, and in some States carried on wholly—in connection with local efforts—by use of a refugees' and freedmen's fund, which had been collected from various sources. Teachers came under the general direction of the assistant commissioners, and protection through the department commanders was given to all engaged in the work.

School superintendents.—Superintendents of schools for each State were appointed July 12, 1865. It was their duty " to work as much as possible in conjunction with State officers who may have had school matters in charge, and to take cognizance of all that was being done to educate refugees and freedmen, secure protection to schools and teachers, promote method and efficiency, and to correspond with the benevolent agencies which were supplying his field."

First general report of inspector.—In September, 1865, your present general superintendent was appointed " inspector of schools." He travelled through nearly all the States lately in insurrection, and made the first general report to the bureau on the subject of education, January 1, 1866.

Extracts from this report give the condition at that time of the freedmen throughout the whole south, with some glimpses of the great work taken in hand, better than any paper which could now be written. He says :

The desire of the freedmen for knowledge has not been overstated. This comes from several causes:

1. The natural thirst for knowledge common to all men.

2. They have seen power and influence among white people always coupled with *learning ;* it is the sign of that elevation to which they now aspire.

3. Its mysteries, hitherto hidden from them in written literature, excites to the special study of *books.*

4. Their freedom has given wonderful stimulus to *all effort,* indicating a vitality which augurs well for their whole future condition and character.

5. But, especially, the practical business of life now upon their hands shows their immediate need of education. This they all feel and acknowledge ; hence their unusual welcome of and attendance upon schools is confined to no one class or age. Those advanced in life throw up their hands at first in despair, but a little encouragement places *even these* as pupils at the alphabet.

Such as are in middle life—the laboring classes—gladly avail themselves of evening and Sabbath schools. They may be often seen during the intervals of toil, when off duty as servants on steamboats, along the railroads, and when unemployed in the streets of the city, or on plantations, with some fragment of a spelling-book in their hands, earnestly at study.

Regiments of colored soldiers have nearly all made improvement in learning. In some of them, where but few knew their letters at first, nearly every man can now read, and many of them write. In other regiments one-half or two-thirds can do this.

Even in hospitals I discovered very commendable efforts at such elementary instruction. But the great movement is among *children* of the *usual school age.* Their parents, if at all intelligent, encourage them to study.

Your officers add their influence, and it is a fact, not always true of children, that among those recently from bondage, the school-house, however rough and uncomfortable, is of all other places most attractive. A very common punishment for misdemeanor is the threat of being *kept at home for a day.* The threat in most cases is sufficient.

Number of schools January 1, 1866.—The total number of pupils at this time, January 1, 1866, in all the colored schools, as near as could be ascertained, was 90,589; teachers, 1,311; schools, 740. In some States numbers had to be put down by general estimate.

Opposition.—The report goes on to say :

Much opposition has been encountered from those who do not believe in the elevation of the negro. A multitude of facts might be given. It is the testimony of all superintendents, that if military power should be withdrawn, our schools would cease to exist.

This opposition is sometimes ludicrous as well as inhuman.

A member of the legislature, in session while I was at New Orleans, was passing one of the schools with me, having, at the time, its recess. The grounds about the building were filled with children. He stopped and looked intently, and then earnestly inquired, "Is *this* a school?" "Yes." I replied. "What! of niggers?" "These are colored children, evidently," I answered. "Well! well!" said he, and raising his hands, "I have seen many an absurdity in my lifetime, but *this is the climax of absurdities!*" I was sure he did not speak for effect, but as he felt. He left me abruptly, and turned the next corner to take his seat with legislators similarly prejudiced.

Petition for schools.—As showing the desire for education among the freedmen, we give the following fact: When the collection of the general tax for colored schools was suspended in Louisiana by military order, the consternation of the colored population was intense. Petitions began to pour in. I saw one from the plantations across the river, at least thirty feet in length, representing ten thousand negroes. It was affecting to examine it, and note the names and marks (×) of such a long list of parents, ignorant themselves, but begging that their children might be educated; promising that from beneath their present burdens and out of their extreme poverty, they would pay for it.

Normal schools wanted.—A class of schools is called for in which colored teachers can be taught. If dignified by the name of "*Normal schools,*" they should commence with training in the simplest elements of the art. Education for the freedmen *as a whole* must be at first very rudimental. The text at present must be mainly in the spelling book; and yet this beginning to be universal. The freedmen all want learning at once. This people are not like pagans in ancient countries who a thousand years hence will be mainly as they are to-day. Slaves, even in a country like this, could not be kept from many noble impulses. The war has been to them a wonderful school of knowledge, of thought, and of purposes; and now suddenly emancipated, these 4,000,000 are as "a nation born in a day."

Education at once, for all.—This great multitude rise up simultaneously, and ask for intelligence. With it they at once start upward in all character. Without it they will as quickly sink into the depravities of ignorance and vice; free to be what they please, and in the presence only of bad example, they will be carried away with every species of evil. And, then, what is the actual and astounding fact? One that startles philanthropy itself. A million, at least, of these four millions, (and mainly the rising generation,) are to-day ready to engage in the study of books. They cannot well be put off. Political, social, financial, and moral considerations all ask that their demand be promptly met. If this million be divided into schools of fifty each, we need for its supply 20,000 teachers. Where are they to come from? The North can supply a few thousand. Perhaps the more noble of the white race here and there in the south will help us. But still at least 15,000 remain to be supplied from some other quarter.

Schools, July 1, 1866.—These, and kindred appeals, had their effect. At the end of the school year, July 1, 1866, it was found that while complete organization had not been reached, the schools in nearly all the States were steadily gaining in numbers, attainment, and general influence. School buildings had been multiplied, teachers showed more aptness and skill in their management and instructions, and pupils continued to make rapid progress. Educational societies were found to have enlarged their patronage and funds, with united agencies of greater efficiency and economy. The disposition of these societies to co-operate heartily with the bureau, accepting its patronage, and adopting its general plans, became apparent.

The official reports of superintendents gave 975 schools, 1,405 teachers, and 90,778 pupils. But these figures were not a true exhibit of the actual increase. They did not include many schools which in that somewhat chaotic period failed to report. It was estimated that, in all the different methods of teaching, there had been during the preceding six months 150,000 freedmen and their children earnestly and successfully occupied in study.

Public sentiment changing—Some change of sentiment had been observed among the better classes of the south; those of higher intelligence acknowledging that education must become universal—planters admitting that it would secure more contented labor. Leading statesmen plead that these millions would be a safer element in their midst, if made moral and intelligent; and religious conventions in many parts of the south passed resolutions urging their membership to give instruction to the negroes.

Still multitudes bitterly opposed the schools. The baser sort had become more brutal than at first; they would not consent to the negro's elevation. He must, in their opinion, remain in every essential respect inferior to themselves. Teachers were proscribed and ill-treated, school-houses burned, and threats so strong that many schools could not be opened; and others, after a brief struggle, had to be closed. Southern men who felt that such outrages were inhuman, thought it not expedient, or had not the moral courage openly to defend the schools, and our correspondence continued to show that only military force for some time to come could prevent the frequent outbreak of every form of violence.

The above statements should be modified as to some of the districts; but this was the general sentiment. It is a marvel how the schools went on. The tenacity and high-souled courage of teachers were admirable. It was more than heroism. There seemed a divine inspiration over the whole work. A creative power had said, "Let there be light."

The country began to feel the moral power of this movement. Commendations of it came from foreign countries, and the universal demand of good men everywhere was that the work should go on.

Bureau continued two years.—On July 16, 1866, the act of Congress to amend the bureau bill, and continue it for the term of two years, was passed in Congress by a two-thirds vote, over the veto of the President.

This bill greatly enlarged the powers of the bureau, especially in regard to education. It sanctioned co-operation with private "benevolent associations, and with agents and teachers duly accredited by them;" and also directed the Commissioner to "hire or provide by lease buildings for purposes of education, whenever teachers and means of instruction, without cost to the government, should be provided." And also, that he should "furnish such protection as might be required for the safe conduct of such schools."

Appropriation for schools.—521,000 dollars were appropriated by Congress in the above bill for school purposes. The bill also provided a considerable fund by the sale or lease of property formerly held by the so-called Confederate States. Other educational expenses, except transportation of teachers, were to be paid out of the fund for refugees and freedmen.

The schools, on the passage of the above act, assumed in all respects a more enlarged and permanent character.

Blanks.—A system of blanks, going into thorough detail, was prepared for teachers, district and State superintendents, and other officers of the bureau. Voluntary associations were requested to report their work on these blanks directly to the bureau. This request was cheerfully complied with, and their enlarged reception of bureau aid cemented mutual obligation.

Graded schools.—Schools in the cities and larger towns began to be graded. Normal or high-schools were planned, and a few came into existence. The earliest of these were at Norfolk, Charleston, New Orleans, and Nashville.

Industrial schools.—Industrial schools for girls, in which were sewing, knitting, straw braiding, &c., having proved a success, were encouraged. School buildings, by rent or construction, were largely provided, and new stimulus was infused into every department.

The whole freed population, in view of new civil rights and what the bureau had undertaken for them, had gained an advanced standing, with increasing self-respect and confidence that a vastly improved condition was within their reach.

Higher branches.—Up to this time it had been questioned whether colored children could advance rapidly into the higher branches. We now found that 23,737 pupils were in writing, 12,970 in geography, 31,692 in arithmetic, and 1,573 in higher branches, and that out of 1,430 teachers of the day and night schools, 458 were colored persons. All doubts as to the ability of colored children to learn, with capacity for higher attainment, were therefore rapidly passing away.

The winter of 1866–'7 proved to be very severe. The poverty of parents, during a number of weeks of the coldest weather, was such they could not provide suitable clothing and shoes for their children. The general attendance of very many schools was diminished, and in others rendered unusually irregular.

Improved school laws were, during the winter, passed by some States, and yet producing but little practical effect; in others there was no movement on the subject, or it was totally defeated.

Rebel theories of reconstruction, and the encouragement given that their views would succeed, brought a variety of other untoward influences to bear upon the education of the colored race.

Progress.—Very decided progress, however, still continued to be made. The January report stated that the actual results reached since these schools commenced, both in numbers and in advancement, were surprising. At the end of the school year, July 1, 1867, it could be said : " We look back with astonishment at the amount accomplished. Such progress as is seen under auspices admitted to be unfavorable, the permanency of the schools, scarcely one failing when once commenced, the rapid increase of general intelligence among the whole colored population, are matters of constant remark by every observer. Thus far this educational effort, considered as a whole, has been eminently successful. The country and the world are surprised to behold a depressed race, so lately and so long in bondage, springing to their feet, and entering the lists in hopeful competition with every rival."

Amount expended during the year 1867.—This bureau had expended during the current fiscal year, which ended October 1, 1867, for all school purposes, $643,766 20; the balance above the appropriation having been taken from the "Freedmen's and Refugee's Fund."

Appropriation for 1867–'8.—The school appropriation for the year to end July, 1868, is $525,000, its use being restricted mainly to transportation of teachers, and rent, repair, and construction of school buildings. It allows, as heretofore, nothing for salaries of teachers, school books, and apparatus, or any incidental expenses. All this is still left for the educational societies to supply.

Consolidation of educational societies.—Great credit is due these societies for their liberality and promptness in meeting the above wants. Their consolidation, with some denominational exceptions, into the two central institutions, the " American Missionary Association " and the " American Freedman's Union Commission," has given great vigor and thoroughness to their co-operation, and produced universal confidence. Their teachers, with scarcely an exception, deserve much credit for ability and unwearied perseverance. We heartily commend them and the institutions they represent to the continued patronage of the benevolent public.

Amount expended from commencement of bureau.—The whole amount expended from the commencement of the bureau to January 1, 1868, for all school purposes, has been $1,066,394 28.

We believe that no public fund was ever used with greater care and economy, nor with more benefit, not only to the freedmen, but to the best interest of the whole southern country. The vast amount of good accomplished cannot be told in mere figures. It has also been in a way to unite the whole popular heart to the work and call out the greatest amount of co-operative effort, volunteer contributions to freedmen's schools being in the aggregate fully equal to the sum expended by this bureau.

This expenditure has been impartial. Refugees and other poor whites of the States lately in rebellion have not been overlooked. In every case where they could be brought into schools it has been done. All parts of the south, city and country, have been explored and equally supplied, as far as possible, with their proportion of these means of instruction.

High and normal schools.—Higher schools, and those for the preparation of teachers, have been aided in equal distribution through the several States. The principal of these, as assisted by the bureau, all of them made permanent institutions by charter of the respective States where they are located, are as follows: National Theological Institute, Washington, D. C.; Howard University, Washington, D. C.; Saint Martin's School, Washington, D. C.; Normal School, Richmond, Virginia; Berea College, Berea, Kentucky; St. Augustine Normal School, Raleigh, North Carolina; Wesleyan College, East Tennessee; Fisk University, Nashville, Tennessee; Storer College, Harper's Ferry, West Virginia; Atlanta University, Atlanta, Georgia; Robert College, Lookout Mountain, Tennessee; Maysville College, Tennessee; Alabama High and Normal Schools; St. Bridget's Parochial School, Pittsburg; South Carolina High and Normal Schools. The total amount given to all these institutions is $168,000.

In view of this brief historical summary, philanthropy and Christian faith need not be disheartened. As we have before remarked, the friends of freedmen should be urged to increasing confidence. Our government will be paid doubly for all its expenditures. We are not making traces in the sand. Hope may grow strong that our work is enduring and shall remain. This people have a vitality which is being aroused from a long, deep, but enforced stupor, and are to have a career in the future which will compensate for all that has been sorrowful or ignoble in their past servitude. Their education should be pushed forward with enthusiasm, with the certainty of great and permanent results.

We now come to the period of our regular report for the six months ending December 31, 1867.

Vacation.—The first three months of this period in most of the schools was vacation, the southern country not permitting unacclimated teachers to remain in safety during the hot season. In some cases however, especially where native teachers were employed, colored or white, there was but a short vacation or none at all. During the month of July 773 schools, day or night, were in operation. In August 528, and in September 639. This does not include 575 Sabbath schools in July, 290 in August, and 362 in September. The eagerness of the freedmen and their children to learn, will make short vacations universal as soon as teachers capable of enduring the climate can be provided.

Depressing influences.—In the early autumn the schools were seriously affected by the alarm of yellow fever. Its fatal prevalence in Texas, and approach along the Gulf coast and lower Mississippi, with the uncertainty as to where it would stop, caused northern teachers to hesitate in resuming their labors. In Louisiana and Mississippi a delay of nearly two months was the consequence.

Still other embarrassments existed. The bloody riots in New Orleans and Memphis had paralyzed efforts for a time in those cities. Intense and universal fear was excited, as life itself seemed no longer sacred.

The failure of the cotton crop followed, and produced general demoralization among both planters and freedmen, materially affecting plans for schools and school-houses; and last, though not least, bitter opposition to the reconstruction of the State governments and interference with elections quite disheartened multitudes of the freedmen. One superintendent reports that "the rebel party, since reconstruction commenced, had broken up a large number of school societies formed among the colored people. Thinking to defeat the new constitutions they devised a plan of changing the negroes from one county to another by starving and threats of violence, and by inducing others to leave the State under the promise of securing for them employment in order to prevent their voting."

These causes combined have had a universally depressing effect, and as the first half of the school year includes the long vacation, with only three months of study, we are not able to report that progress which those unacquainted with the facts might anticipate.

The statistics thus far, however, are larger than those of the corresponding months of the previous year, showing, after all, a steady and irresistable growth of school interest among the freedmen. Nothing, as we believe, will suppress it. It can be satisfied only by ministrations equal to its demand. The benevolent who give must persevere, the government should still be liberal, and the States where these freedmen dwell, seeing how their own best welfare is involved, will soon, we hope, take up the matter in earnest and provide liberally for universal education.

Benevolent associations.—The benevolent associations have undertaken to do an equal amount and more, if possible, than last year. They are now better organized than ever, with superintendents and teachers of increased experience. Their patrons throughout the country show no abatement of zeal; though under great pressure from every quarter, they respond liberally to the continuous calls made upon them.

State school laws.—Much is expected from the constitutions now being framed by conventions of the several southern States. Excellent provision by those already in session is being made for the equal education of *all children* and setting apart funds adequate thereto. If the people ratify these constitutions there will be immediate organization of State systems with efficient superintendents, and this work will fall into its legitimate and proper channels. These States will then be enabled gradually to assume what the general government and the benevolent of the north have been doing for them, with results doubtless far more satisfactory to all concerned. Aid from without will, we hope, be given through the transition process, and as long as it shall be actually needed.

Future prospects.—Should this bureau be continued and the public measures now in progress for the well-being of freedmen be consummated, results far greater than heretofore will soon be witnessed. We are no longer obliged to argue "ability to learn" on the part of the negro race. Schools in large numbers, highly successful and of all grades, are in actual operation. A great process is going on, not of experiment but of unceasingly productive results. A little more time and the full development of *an institution* will appear. This formative process will crystallize into fixed, unalterable shape; the movement now so complicated will have evolved a harmonious, perfect whole, and on ground never before occupied by a common school system. Then we shall have a finished edifice worthy of those who have labored in its construction, and for which those who now oppose us will be forever grateful.

Normal schools.—Attention should again be called to the endowment of normal schools. Teachers trained on the ground is the urgent want of the present moment; those of whatever color who will be identified with the people, to grow into and become themselves part of the community they are forming; those who will take the schools as teachers *by profession*, carrying them with only the ordinary vacation through the entire year, and through year after year; acting with steady, elevating influence upon the whole mass of the people, introducing culture into home life, a pure morality into every circle, thus perfecting solid, permanent, and virtuous society.

These normal schools, so far as they are in existence, already win universal favor. The educational associations are using their funds in founding them on the broadest basis. Private individuals are bestowing liberal endowments, and the bureau has appropriated, during only the last year, $59,000 for the erection of suitable buildings, besides giving transportation and other aid to their teachers.

We take the liberty of giving in a single view the educational work of this bureau, for the period now reported, throughout the whole field. The following consolidated table shows not only the aggregate but the relative work in each of the southern States. Its substance will be recapitulated in the reports from each State separately.

Consolidated school report to Bureau of Refugees, Freedmen and

	Delaware.	Maryland.	Dist. of Columbia.	Virginia.	North Carolina.	South Carolina.	Georgia.	Florida.
Day schools	19	77	81	175	126	45	77	66
Night schools	8	18	4	32	42		19	1
Total	27	95	85	207	168	45	96	67
Amount of tuition paid by freedmen	$386 40	$5,823 20		$3,784 04	$4,776 87	$3,467 65	$1,700 00	$250 00
Amount of expense by bureau for 6 months		16 66	$14,985 43	11,930 59	13,713 96	2,062 67	250 00	
Total cost of support of schools by all parties.	1,350 00	9,864 00	12,953 00	27,392 11	28,484 41	17,000 00		10 00
Schools sustained by freedmen	1	20	2	43	52	5	49	13
Schools sustained in part by freedmen	20	61	58	48	38	25	42	3
Teachers transported by bureau	25	95	50	225	89	26	78	16
School buildings own'd by freedmen	7	67	10	44	63	4	27	7
School buildings furnished by bureau	11	21	46	71	42	26	5	2
Teachers: White	10	36	89	163	106	84	95	30
Colored	18	86	26	89	71	35	30	26
Total	28	122	115	252	177	119	125	56
Pupils enrolled, both day and night schools:								
Male	468	2,403	2,380	5,878	5,137	3,133	2,997	1,512
Female	490	2,495	2,203	6,572	5,083	3,610	3,083	1,543
Total	958	4,898	4,583	12,450	10,220	6,743	6,088	3,085
Average attendance	709	3,404	3,650	8,794	7,206	5,315	4,493	904
Pupils paying tuition	888	3,163	245	2,801	2,497	335	1,373	246
White pupils		2	29	655	234	5	4	40
Always present	658	2,153	2,153	5,612	4,537	3,180	2,652	464
Always punctual	572	2,413	1,415	5,052	4,385	3,216	2,423	532
Over 16 years of age	271	578	614	2,637	2,709	745	1,007	209
In alphabet	123	448	557	1,494	828	1,983	1,186	258
Spell & read easy less'ns	495	1,702	2,393	4,979	4,595	2,213	2,962	627
Advanced readers	268	1,755	1,765	4,870	2,998	3,217	1,556	283
Geography	178	1,258	2,354	4,157	2,262	2,338	1,449	183
Arithmetic	377	2,242	2,924	5,919	3,148	3,708	2,144	303
Higher branches	22	292	383	1,281	514	342	100	158
Writing	410	2,192	2,501	6,033	3,397	3,007	1,907	279
Needle work	13	404	262	403	304	339	142	37
Free before the war	958	783	2,851	680	1,288	813	360	91
Sabbath schools	15	39	21	136	99	31	54	27
Teachers in Sab. schools	61	243		601	529		100	
Pupils in Sab. schools	1,000	2,217	2,296	7,768	8,485	2,788	5,410	1,046
Graded schools		20	61	87	33	20	32	8
How many grades		2	3	3	2	3	4	4
Day or night schools not regularly reported		23	23	14	60	55	12	23
Teachers: White		8	28	6	10	20	6	
Colored		19	12	40	52	45	6	35
Total		27	40	46	62	65	12	35
Estimated No. of pupils Sabbath schools not regularly reported		630	1,205	1,099	2,249	5,000	305	764
		145		39	75	70	10	6
Teachers: White		457		100	33	50		48
Colored		768		160	242	130		40
Total		1,225		200	275	180		88
Estimated No. of pupils		9,847		3,443	4,534	7,000	595	697
Industrial schools		15	6	5	1		1	2
Pupils in same		480	340	400	123		30	
High or normal schools	2	4	2	2	1	2	3	
Pupils in same	86	181	77	101	28	500	100	

Abandoned Lands for the six months ending January 1, 1868.

Alabama.	Mississippi.	Louisiana.	Texas.	Arkansas.	Tennessee.	Kentucky.	Missouri and Kansas.	Total.
58	55	148	18	16	102	107	28	1,198
12	21	70	16	2	25	13	5	288
70	76	218	34	18	127	120	33	1,486
....	$1,692 86	$28,943 10	$464 00	$1,470 80	$5,663 83	$6,897 00	....	$65,319 75
....	1,060 51	3,694 55	1,628 32	516 75	10,283 19	5,364 99	$1,700 86	67,208 48
....	4 809 33	32,637 65	2,092 92	4,481 25	25,034 86	13,334 91	803 60	180,247 44
1	7	191	6	7	32	39	1	469
8	47	7	18	11	49	78	18	531
9	39	21	....	9	147	48	2	879
6	12	17	11	10	37	41	1	364
18	20	28	6	7	30	75	9	417
68	50	106	19	19	93	33	39	1,031
15	25	85	13	12	47	112	20	713
83	75	191	32	31	140	145	53	1,744
2,082	1,953	3,715	565	486	2,880	3,048	1,233	39,909
2,353	1,943	3,476	566	520	3,283	3,445	1,304	41,969
4,435	3,896	7,191	1,133	1,006	6,172	6,493	2,537	81,878
3,209	1,885	6,156	648	771	4,562	5,230	1,806	58,790
303	906	5,096	511	346	2,903	3,973	413	26,139
4	5	35	1	10	11	80	23	1,138
2,608	1,543	5,666	658	495	3,153	4,669	1,287	41,553
2,670	1,385	4,019	642	463	3,018	4,545	1,186	37,926
443	714	1,153	129	143	1,064	685	282	13,377
705	237	1,439	105	101	761	1,058	545	11,131
2,611	1,448	2,926	265	724	2,926	3,073	930	34,969
1,119	1,706	1,993	420	233	2,533	2,012	1,190	27,980
457	905	1,479	155	156	1,956	1,169	574	21,032
796	1,472	2,009	401	375	2,687	1,977	1,657	31,539
91	114	274	34	60	417	348	245	4,675
836	1,541	2,019	511	400	2,155	2,125	1,254	30,567
....	7	40	4	43	195	56	42	2,381
10	30	32	88	14	161	357	28	8,743
26	42	86	5	16	66	83	26	772
....	....	93	....	41	356	....	78	2,105
2,665	2,845	4,319	394	1,625	6,178	6,343	1,798	57,177
....	4	19	7	1	45	35	....	372
....	4	3	3	3	4	3	....	
....	10	63	26	7	20	8	45	389
....	5	28	13	8	5	3	....	140
....	7	53	17	2	15	15	....	318
....	12	81	30	10	20	18	....	458
....	477	2,226	689	295	600	480	2,550	18,589
....	4	25	7	10	....	7	....	398
....	3	13	7	11	....	3	....	725
....	43	86	6	11	....	34	....	1,460
....	46	99	13	22	....	37	....	2,185
....	569	2,067	515	400	....	664	....	30,270
....	....	....	....	1	....	....	....	39
....	....	....	....	35	8	....	....	1,603
....	1	1	....	....	105	6	1	25
....	127	132	....	....	180	225	....	1,737

Grand total : Schools of all kinds, 3,084 ; teachers, 6,492 ; pupils, 189,517.

It will be seen from the above table that there are regularly reported 1,486 day or night schools, with 1,744 teachers and 81,878 pupils ; 772 Sabbath schools, with 2,105 teachers and 57,177 pupils ; and 39 industrial schools, with 1,603 pupils.

Twenty-five of the above are high or normal schools.

There are also " within the knowledge of the superintendents, but not regularly reported," 389 day or night schools, with 458 teachers and 18,589 pupils ; and 398 Sabbath schools, with 2,185 teachers and 30,270 pupils. Schools of all kinds, 3,084 ; teachers, 6,492 ; pupils, 189,517. Of the whole number of schools 1,000 are sustained wholly or in part by the freedmen, and they own 364 of the buildings used for school purposes.

Two thousand nine hundred and forty-eight teachers are white and 3,544 colored. Transportation has been furnished by the bureau to 879 of these teachers.

Twenty-six thousand one hundred and thirty-nine pupils have paid tuition, amounting in the aggregate to $65,319 75, or within a fraction of $2 50 per scholar. The average attendance in the day and night schools has been 58,790, or over 71 per cent. of the enrolment.

This bureau has expended for rents, repairs and construction of school buildings during the last six months, $361,205 48 ; and for other educational purposes during the same period, $97,201 67 ; making a total of $458,407 15.

This amount includes the $67,208 48, as reported by State superintendents.

The whole amount expended for the support of the above schools by all parties during the last half year has been $571,446 11.

As showing the advancement of pupils, 21,032 are studying geography, 31,539 arithmetic, 30,567 are in writing, and 4,675 are in the higher branches.

These statistics indicate that, though encountering many difficulties, the schools are moving steadily onward. Their diminished numbers we have accounted for above.

Summer vacation.—The long summer vacation, among such a people as this, is, of itself, sadly disorganizing. After it the beginning of each fall term has always shown an attendance either greatly diminished or very irregular. The Christmas holidays were over this year before the schools began to assume anything like their full proportions. From the present date we shall expect a showing equal, at least, to that of last year, and hope greatly to exceed it.

DISTRICT OF COLUMBIA, WEST VIRGINIA, AND PORTION OF MARYLAND—GENERAL C. H. HOWARD, ASSISTANT COMMISSIONER.

In this department, where some of the oldest schools for freedmen are located, the effect of instruction is most apparent. The bureau, as always present, has acted with great energy. Educational agencies have accomplished around our national capital a work full of credit to themselves and their patrons. Extreme ignorance among that multitude of colored people who flocked to this great centre as to an asylum after the war, has been exchanged for comparative intelligence. Their former servile spirit has largely given place to self-respect. The marriage relation is now stamped with sacredness. Home life with its blessings begins to appear. The rising generation are taught to commence with high aims, and multitudes of these children have acquired a vast amount of elementary knowledge.

Sabbath and night schools, for moral training and teaching of adults, have added very important results to those of the day schools. There are, indeed, many exceptions, as with all communities, in the direction of vice. But with suffrage in the hands of freedmen, as it has been for some time in this District, they are manly in its exercise without exhibition of turbulence, and as a community are temperate, orderly, quiet, and, so far as labor can be had, are remarkably industrious.

Agencies engaged.—The agencies engaged in this District have been more varied than elsewhere. Besides the educational societies, associations, churches, and individuals from abroad, to whom warmest gratitude is due, there has been a vast amount of local effort both associated and personal. Individuals from the churches and Christian Association, with good men from the state departments, have labored during their spare hours with untiring zeal. That "clerks occupying government desks are good for nothing else," we know to be an unfounded scandal in the case of a large number of these public employés. Many of them have a philanthropic and Christian record which, if known, would insure them wide respect and honor. Their toils and sacrifices for the freedmen in this District during the last six years have called down many a blessing upon their heads from " those who were ready to perish."

It should be said that the colored population formerly free have co-operated very fully in school efforts. The wealthier among them have carried on their former educational work more vigorously than ever, and without aid from government ; while the poorer class have shared the benefits of the free schools with the same elevating effect as experienced by the freedmen ; and they have also participated in all the material aid granted by the government through the bureau.

Savings bank.—As showing the general drift of prosperity among the colored population of Washington, we can state that they had on deposit in their branch of the savings bank January 1, 1868, $59,470 08, and that these deposits are from month to month rapidly increasing.

The effect of national institutions for the colored people centred at the capital, like this savings bank and the university now being founded here, is to inspire a common effort to rise, and with confidence in the government thus endeavoring to elevate them.

Summary.—In this whole department there are officially reported for the last six months 85 schools, 115 teachers, 4,583 pupils ; 2,891 of these pupils are paying tuition, 50 of the teachers have been transported by this bureau, and 10 of the school buildings are owned by the freedmen themselves, while they sustain wholly or in part 60 of the schools. Of these schools 61 are graded, ranging from one to three.

Twenty-one Sabbath schools are reported with an attendance of 2,296 pupils.
High or normal schools two, pupils 77.

Industrial schools six, pupils 340.

There are also, " within the knowledge of the superintendent " and "not regularly reported," 23 day or night schools, with 40 teachers, and 1,205 pupils, making a grand total of

Schools of all kinds 135
Pupils 8, 424

The bureau has expended during the last six months for the support of the above schools $11,985 43.

The assistant commissioner for this department in his full and interesting annual report says :

The schools are in a flourishing condition, with special plans and efforts to increase their numbers, particularly in the rural districts, and the benevolent societies have assisted liberally in sustaining the work during the past year.

The chief expenditure of the bureau has been in rentals and repairs of buildings ; the repairs being mainly in fitting up school rooms in government barracks. Sixty-two schools, averaging 50 scholars each, have been thus provided for during the past year, at a cost of about $7,000. Many of the night schools, also, have been held in the same buildings.

A considerable expense has been incurred for school furniture, including desks, chairs, and stoves.

The transportation of teachers to and from their homes—the greater part in distant States—is an item of large expense in this District.

Most of the schools in the District are now comfortably provided with school-houses

During the present term some government buildings will be used, and rent for a few rooms, chiefly for night schools for adults, will be paid by the bureau; after that, the probabilities are that all expenses will be paid out of the public school fund. The trustees of the colored schools for the cities of Washington and Georgetown have, during the year, paid the salaries of ten teachers and about $5,000 of incidental expenses.

Superintendent's report.—The superintendent of education, Reverend John Kimball, reports, for the month of October, that there was paid for material furnished for the building of 15 school-houses, the sum of $6,709 45; for repairs, $1,312 25.

The number of teachers, and, therefore, the number of scholars thus far in the term now commenced, are not as large as last year.

Some of the northern societies withdrew their teachers from Washington in expectation that the city would support a sufficient number of schools without their aid. This will be done if efforts to obtain the public money, now due, succeeds. In that case the number of teachers will be increased and the societies relieved permanently from further care of the schools in this city.

Five industrial schools are reported: four in this city and one at Freedmen's village. All the material for work in four of them has been furnished by the bureau, at a cost, for the month, of $2,352 25. The amount paid by the bureau to teachers and women who sew in these schools, for the month, was $805 67. Seventy of the scholars receive rations and clothing. Two thousand and seventy-nine garments have been made in October, and 110 yards of braid. Nearly all the garments are turned over to the local superintendent for this bureau, who distributes them among the needy.

For November, the superintendent reports that there was paid for material and labor furnished for the building of 15 school-houses $2,948 62.

There are 1,065 scholars more than was reported for the month of October. Great difficulty is found in getting good teachers, or societies to pay their salaries, in the country districts.

Six industrial schools are now in operation, in which 340 persons are enrolled, 101 of whom receive rations. There has been paid towards one industrial building $546 75.

For the months of October, November, and December, 1867, bills, amounting to $14,985 43, were paid by this bureau for school purposes.

City buildings.—In the cities of Washington and Georgetown, the bureau, with aid from the city governments, has erected six valuable school-houses some of them of brick, and two large enough for eight schools each, all on sites for which a deed to special trustees has been taken. This makes the whole number of school-houses built on the above plan in this department 56. Such permanent building, on soil secured to the colored people *forever* for educational purposes, is the first and most important thing to be done in every place where a school is needed.

Industrial schools.—These had little to do through the preceding summer. But the distress among women and children, for want of employment, has been much greater thus far during the present winter than at any previous time. The number has been daily increasing by destitute families from the country, who come in as a last resort from extreme suffering and death.

In the months of October, November, and December, the industrial schools were in operation nearly all the time. The following is a list of these, with the names of their teachers, viz:

School at Wisewell barracks, taught by Miss Susan Walker; school at corner Twenty-second and I streets, taught by Mrs. S. C. Tumey; school at corner Seventeenth and I streets, taught by Mrs. L. M. E. Ricks; school at North Capitol street, taught by Mrs. J. S. Griffing; school at East Capitol street barracks, taught by Miss Harriett Carter; school at Freedmen's village, taught by Miss Eliza Heacock.

All these are in buildings provided by the bureau. Fuel is also furnished.

The material manufactured into garments has been purchased by the bureau for all the schools except Miss Carter's and Miss Walker's; they have been supplied in good part by northern friends. Amount paid by the bureau for new material, $3,182 85; the average number of persons employed each month is 340 ; whole number of garments manufactured, 6,582; amount paid in money for their manufacture, $2,155 62. Over 70 of those employed have also received rations all the time. These garments have been distributed to the destitute during the winter months by the local superintendent of the bureau. A large and well-arranged building has been erected for the industrial school taught by Miss Walker.

The object of these schools is to furnish employment for indigent colored women, and to instruct them in sewing and other branches of housework. In some of the schools lessons are also given in reading and writing. Very rapid progress is reported as being made in learning the branches taught.

An industrial school for girls at Wirewell Barracks, taught by a volunteer association of ladies, promises well.

WEST VIRGINIA.

In West Virginia there is an impartial system of free schools, but those of color are required to be separate, and the execution of the law is entirely in the hands of the whites. Some dozen of our teachers have been paid from their public school fund, which the law requires to be expended impartially for whites and blacks.

Plan for school-houses.—An excellent and permanent work has been undertaken in this department in the construction of school-houses. The plan is specially intended to awaken an interest in education among the colored people themselves. Meetings on the subject have been held in each of the Maryland counties, addressed by distinguished speakers, in which the freed people at once take great interest, some of them walking 20 miles to be present. A portion of the time is devoted to explaining the manner in which the aid of the bureau can be obtained in establishing a school in the place. The conditions required are as follows : there should be at least thirty scholars; a site must be secured by deed to trustees—generally colored—for a free school forever ; the colored people are to raise by subscription funds sufficient to construct the house, and agree to pay the board of the teacher. The bureau then will supply the lumber, and sometimes all the material, and also, in behalf of one of the educational societies, engages to send a teacher, whose salary shall be paid for at least one term. When a site is donated, as has been done in several instances by friendly whites, the bureau pays for a portion only of the material.

The following are the results in the Maryland counties, viz :

School-houses completed.. 29
School houses in process of erection.............................. 12
                                                                  ———
    Total... 41

The offer of the bureau to the freed people in West Virginia is similar to that in Maryland, except that the co-operation of the school board of the township is secured and the deed of the site made to it ; and, as there is always under the law something due from the public school fund, the amount promised by the bureau is limited to $200 for most places. In some of the more populous towns a greater amount is given in order to insure the erection of larger buildings.

The following has been the result in West Virginia:

School-houses completed... 4
School-houses now in process of erection............................ 5
                                                                     ——
Total.. 9
                                                                     ——
Total school-houses built in Maryland and West Virginia........ 50
                                                                     ══

We desire to commend the above plan to all the States south. It secures a permanent school in every place where one is attempted. The freedmen are fully committed to the enterprise by having to bear a portion of the responsibility and expense. While their white friends are allowed to help, which they often do by donating a site and other aid, the furnishing of a teacher for the first year by some benevolent society will, in most cases it is believed, carry the school beyond the need of further assistance.

The following is the form of deed used in securing the above object :

This deed, made this —— day of ———, in the year eighteen hundred and ——, by —— ———, witnesseth, that, in consideration of the sum of ———, the said —— ——— do— grant unto —— ———, in trust, for the purpose of erecting or allowing to be erected thereon a school-house, for the use, benefit, and education of the colored people of ——— county, forever, all that lot or parcel of ground lying in ——— county which is described as follows : beginning for the same ———.

Witness my hand and seal.

[SEAL.]   —— ——.

Attest:

—— ——.

MARYLAND AND DELAWARE.

Maryland and Delaware, though not States lately in rebellion, have an interesting freed population, and both have received assistance from the bureau, the former, very largely.

Returns from this department are encouraging. Thus early in the term there are 359 schools of all kinds and 20,030 pupils. Of these 122 are day and night schools regularly reported, with 150 teachers, (46 white and 104 colored,) and 5,856 pupils ; 54 Sabbath schools, with 304 teachers and 3,217 pupils ; 15 industrial schools, with 480 pupils ; and 6 high or normal schools, with 267 pupils.

Schools "not regularly reported," but "within the knowledge of the superintendent," are as follows : Day and night schools 23, with 27 teachers and 630 pupils ; Sabbath schools 145, with 1,225 teachers and 9,847 pupils.

Of the above schools 102 are sustained wholly or in part by the freedmen ; and they own 74 of the buildings in which these schools are kept.

Four thousand and fifty-one pupils in the day and night schools pay tuition, the aggregate amount for the six months being $6,209 60, or $1 53 per scholar.

Expenditure by all parties for the support of the above schools for the past six months has been $9,864.

This bureau has furnished 120 of the teachers with transportation.

The assistant commissioner, Major General E. M. Gregory, reported in October that—

Mr. William Howard Day, the new school superintendent, seems to be fully up to the mark, and has taken hold of the work of education in good earnest.

During the vacation strenuous efforts have been made to finish school-houses in time for the usual opening of schools in October.

Baltimore.—In the city of Baltimore the schools are now in charge of the city councils, and have been re-numbered and classified anew as nearly as possible. The city superintendent will co-operate with us cheerfully and promptly for the interests of the freedmen.

Efforts are being made to induce a stronger attendance of the children of freedmen in this city, as the present attendance is by no means in proportion to the number of children reported in the last census. This is imperatively necessary to secure to them the advantages of education in the present aspect of affairs.

The success of the past year is most encouraging. The colored people have become intensely interested, and the school, after a long vacation, began more hopefully than ever before. A spirit is abroad which needs only to be fostered to soon render them self-sustaining.

The great want.—The great want of the freed people is the school-house and teachers. The demand far exceeds the supply. We ought now to have 300 teachers in the field instead of but one-third that number. But to meet this demand funds will be needed, and the benevolence of the Christian public of this country appealed to in the past, and never appealed to in vain, must continue to assist in this great work.

Already many of those who were opposed to the extension of educational privileges to the colored people begin to see that these advantages are not incompatible with earnest industry and honest labor, and that the best interests of the community are subserved by care for the interest of this class.

We therefore enter upon a new year with full faith that the anticipations indulged will yet be realized, and that the States of Maryland and Delaware will not be long behind sister States in the march of education and improvement.

The Baltimore association for the moral and educational improvement of the colored people continue their efficient co-operation.

In December the assistant commissioner says :

Educational effort now reaches the most remote parts of this district. The last report shows more pupils enrolled than in any previous month since April.

The Baltimore schools, as appears from the certificate appended, while carried on by the city council, are now all to report to this bureau.

"OFFICE OF THE COMMISSIONER PUBLIC SCHOOLS,
" *Baltimore, October,* 1867.

" This certifies that the board of commissioners of public schools of the city of Baltimore have directed the teachers of the colored schools under their charge to report monthly to William Howard Day, esq., superintendent of colored schools for the State of Maryland.
" By order :

" W. D. McJILTON,
" *Secretary Board of Commissioners Public Schools.*"

The city superintendent reports these schools, "Never in so efficient a condition as now." In addition to two private or independent schools reported in last quarter Mr. Day has obtained reports from 19 others, many of them in a high state of efficiency.

The Baltimore night schools are conducted by teachers detailed from day schools by order of the school board. The normal school in Baltimore is now occupying convenient rooms, which were formally opened December 16, with public exercises.

Throughout this district the freedmen have been urged to make their schools self-supporting, and I am pleased to report that 50 schools in Maryland have agreed to pay each twelve dollars per month towards a fund to be used in opening new schools.

Change for the better.—Public sentiment in the district is changing for the better. No personal violence has been offered to teachers during the quarter. An unfinished building was burned in Delaware. It was intended for both a school and church. Indifference seems to be the best description now of public feeling, and this we regard as progress.

In two instances in Cecil county the public school money has been returned to the colored people by the county commissioners, and assurances have been given that their schools will be taken under the fostering care of the county.

Delaware.—The colored people of Delaware have contributed during the past year to the cause of education $1,959 25, of which amount $3,327 84 was for the erection of school houses of the material furnished by this bureau. The total estimated value of said buildings is $10,233 92.

In Wilmington the normal schools are fully established and are steadily progressing.

A report of the Delaware association has just reached us, from which we are happy to make the following extracts. It is a more full account than we have been able heretofore to give of what Delaware is doing :

The first meeting of the association was held on the 27th day of December, 1866. After interesting addresses by Judge Bond and Francis T. King, of Baltimore, and Major General Gregory, of the Freedmen's Bureau, it was resolved by those present to organize forthwith an association for the moral improvement and education of the colored people of the State.

A draught of a constitution was presented and adopted, and the board then chosen met on the 9th of January, 1867, for effective operations.

An earnest appeal from the pen of Bishop Lee was now issued, invoking the co-operation and active assistance of the community on our behalf. The address says:

"We need not inform you that this large class of our population are wholly excluded from the benefit of our system of public education, although not exempt from taxation, in some shape, for the public schools. While legislation thus closes against them the avenues of knowledge and improvement, it has visited in their case the crimes and offences which naturally flow from ignorance and degradation with excessive and cruel penalties. Persistence in such glaring injustice must be attended with grave accountability, for, in the providence of a righteous God, every wrong brings, sooner or later, its retribution.

"May we not hope that the following considerations will commend themselves to your judgment, and secure for this effort your sympathy and co-operation:

" 1. The manifest equity of no longer excluding any class of our community from those advantages of knowledge and mental culture upon which we set so high a value. To those who doubt their capacity for improvement, we say, give them, at any rate, the opportunity.

" 2. The rescue of a large number of the young from indolence, profligacy, and vice, to which they are now so much exposed.

" 3. The general social improvement which may be expected to attend the moral elevation of the immediate subjects of our labor, for an influence emanates from every class to raise or depress the standard of intelligence and good conduct.

" 4. The certain benefits to productive industry—benefits that will be felt in many pursuits and in various ways. The instructed, skilful, and well-conditioned laborer is a far more valuable member of the commonwealth than the ignorant, stolid, and thriftless.

" 5. The satisfaction of doing something to redress a great wrong, and to pay a debt long overdue to the poor and defenceless."

These sentiments are noble and just and from the right source.

About this time a general agent, John G. Furey, was appointed by the executive committee, with an office at 815 Market street, Wilmington.

The results accomplished are as follows:

The association took charge of the 12th street school, Wilmington, which for several years had been sustained by private contribution. It has numbered, on an average, about 50 pupils in attendance.

A school at Dover was opened on the 11th of February, 1867, under the charge of Joseph H. Rodgers, a graduate of the colored institute at Philadelphia, Pennsylvania.

Following in rapid succession schools were opened at Seaford, Smyrna, Christiana, Odessa, Milford, Laurel, Georgetown, New Castle, Milton, Newark, Delaware City, Lewis, Camden, Newport, Williamsville, and Port Penn, besides another school at Wilmington in the school room of the Zion African church. Most of these schools have been conducted successfully, and to the satisfaction of the managers.

Two other schools established in Wilmington claim a more special notice.

The African School Association placed at our disposal their premises on Orange street, and the income of their funds: the conditions being simply that the Delaware Association should establish and maintain, on said premises, as high an order of schools for the colored people as their condition permitted.

These schools, after considerable expenditure by the Freedmen's Bureau in enlarging and altering the building to accommodate them, have been opened the past season under the name of normal schools, and although the present advancement of the pupils hardly justifies the use of such a title, yet the managers hope that, by persevering effort, the intellectual standard and mental training of the scholars may gradually progress, until we shall, at no distant day, be able to send forth annually graduating classes of young colored men and women properly qualified as teachers of their race, and thus scatter over the land not only the best fruits of our own oversight and care, but also the most beneficent results of the charity founded by the original donors of the funds and property of the African School Society.

The managers would make a public acknowledgment of the vast service rendered by the Freedmen's Bureau to the cause of education among the colored people of Delaware.

Especially would they desire to record their appreciation of the zeal and fidelity of Major General Gregory, in promoting, on all occasions, the objects of this association.

About $12,000 have been collected and expended in the operations of the association during the past year, besides over $10,000 furnished in material by the Freedmen's Bureau.

The whole care.—It is expected that Maryland and Delaware will soon be left mainly to take the whole care of these freedmen's schools, as most of the bureau agents will soon be withdrawn from those States. The work is well begun, and it may be presumed that a people so abounding in intelligence and wealth will be not only able but willing to educate their whole population.

The superintendent, in concluding his report, says :

I enter upon another quarter more full of hope than ever. I have been received every-where with marked courtesy, and I may say with kindness, by persons of all classes.

Through God's blessing, and bureau help, the colored people will lift themselves from the depression of bondage and proscription to the light, the duties, and the privileges of intelligent freedmen.

VIRGINIA.

Schools for freedmen were opened at a very early period in Virginia, furnishing a model for States further south, and they still maintain a first rank and move steadily onward.

From the statistical reports of the superintendent we are enabled to make the following statement of those in session during the last six months :

Summary.—Day and night schools 207, with 252 teachers and 12,450 pupils. The average attendance has been 70 per cent. Sabbath schools, 136, with 601 teachers and 7,768 pupils. Industrial schools, 5 ; pupils, 400. High or normal schools, 2 ; pupils, 101.

Of the above schools, 87 are graded, being primary, intermediate, and grammar. There are 14 day and night schools, " not regularly reported," with an attendance of 1,099 pupils, and taught by 46 teachers ; 39 Sabbath schools, with 200 teachers and 3,442 pupils.

Tuition has been paid by 2,891 of the pupils in the day and night schools, the amount of which has been $3,784 04, or about $1 31 per scholar. The grand total of schools of all kinds is 401 ; pupils, 25,159.

Transportation has been furnished by this bureau to 225 of the teachers in the day and night schools. The bureau has expended for rents, materials, and repairs of the above schools during the six months $11,930 59 ; whole expense by all parties for the same period, $27,392 11.

Excellent scholars, even from the class who began with the alphabet, are now found in the schools of this State. A healthy stimulus is infused into all of them, the example of the oldest and most advanced being strongly felt by those of more recent date, and the preparation of teachers from promising colored youth now in process of education has become an object of great interest with the associations laboring here.

Normal schools.—Two normal schools are in successful operation ; one at Hampton and the other at Richmond—both with appropriate buildings, already erected, and each preparing to graduate classes of thorough professional teachers. An account of these schools is given elsewhere.

The colored people of Virginia are fixed in the determination to have education for their children.

The following letter shows the sacrifices they are willing to make. It is from the interior of the State :

Dear Sir: I have this day forwarded an application for transportation for two teachers. I have been acquainted with them for the past 18 years. I was agreeably surprised to know that our friends would send me teachers, as I had given up all hope of getting any more from any source. The freedmen are so anxious to learn that they will divide their means equally between their children's bread and their education. There will be no trouble about the teachers' board or rooms. The colored people here have very near enough money raised already to pay the board, and are only waiting for the rooms to be rented or leased and the teachers to come. Each teacher will have from 60 to 125 scholars, if they can possibly teach so many. Sixty is the lowest average, I believe, and as many more will come as the teacher will allow to do so.

I respectfully ask that you will crowd the matter ahead as a particular favor to these poor unfortunate freedmen.

I am yours, very respectfully,

GEO. W. GRAHAM,
Acting Sub-Assistant Commissioner.

Superintendent of Education, *Richmond, Virginia.*

The assistant commissioner, General O. Brown, has forwarded a full account of the educational work in this State. Nothing need be added to encourage its friends to move hopefully forward. We give a few extracts :

The results of the educational labors of the year are, in every point of view, full of interest and encouragement.

From the statistics of the schools and from other data it will appear that a larger number of persons has been brought under instruction than during any like period before, and that the facilities for primary and higher branches have been increased, the prejudice and hostility towards public schools for the freedmen largely overcome, and a general expectation created of the early establishment of a system of public free schools at the expense of the State. This expectation is universal among the freed people, and its full accomplishment is waited for with increasing impatience.

The whole number of different pupils who have received instruction, either in our public free schools or in the numerous small private schools, cannot be less than 25,000. It is impossible to obtain statements precisely accurate of this private and voluntary instruction. Such schools, however, are rapidly increasing.

An interesting fact appears from the average attendance as compared with the whole number of pupils. This has been almost identical with that given in the last annual school reports of Connecticut, Massachusetts, and Vermont, viz: 70 per cent.

During the year about 8,000 children have passed through the primary steps, embracing the alphabet and primer; about 10,000 have been added to the intelligent reading population of the State; an equal number are respectably advanced in geography and arithmetic, and many have made good progress in grammar, history of the United States, and algebra.

Capacity of pupils.—It has been a question in the minds of many friends of these schools whether the pupils would not decline in good scholarship in proportion as they advanced in studies requiring more particularly the exercise of the reflective and reasoning faculties. No such indications appear in the highest classes of our advanced schools; on the contrary, these are the most promising and encouraging of all.

The number of teachers supported by the various educational agencies at the north is but a little short of 200, the average expense of their support being $500 each per annum. The whole expenditure upon the schools, as derived from these charities, has been about $100,000.

The most conclusive evidence of a change of public sentiment for the better is found in the fact that applications from native Virginians, of respectable social position, for employment as teachers in the colored schools are becoming common, and a considerable number of this class have established schools for freedmen in different parts of the State; in some instances with the assistance of the bureau, and in others independent of it.

Liberality of freedmen.—In rural localities the freedmen have liberally contributed their labor, and sometimes money and material, in the erection of school-houses. The extent of this assistance will be seen from the fact that 45 school-houses have been erected at an average cost to the bureau of only $130 each, making $5,850 in all. So great has been the impatience in several places to possess school-houses that the freedmen have erected buildings without aid from the bureau and without any immediate prospect of enjoying the services of a teacher.

The various charitable associations have conducted their operations with great energy and liberality. Extensive and beneficial as their work has been, it is, however, only an introduction to that yet to be undertaken, and which, in its magnitude, is beyond the reach of charity and the present appropriation of the bureau, for the purpose.

There is an immediate demand for not less than 200 additional teachers and school-houses. To meet fully the educational wants of the colored population of the State, 1,500 teachers are required to instruct the 75,000 pupils who would be in daily attendance.

Increase of colored population.—The census of the colored population of the State, although still imperfect, shows it to be greater than before the war, notwithstanding the constant assertions by many that the race is dying out.

Important progress has been made in providing training schools for colored teachers to meet this demand.

A handsome and thoroughly-appointed normal school building has been completed in the city of Richmond, and will immediately go into operation. Schools with similar aims will soon be in progress in Norfolk, Hamilton, Alexandria, and Danville. It is hoped that these will, to a considerable extent, supply the greatest want of the future, viz: a class of competent teachers, who can afford to live and labor among their own people for a very moderate compensation.

NORTH CAROLINA.

Down to 1835 the free negroes of this State, numbering between 30,000 and 40,000, were permitted to establish and maintain schools for the education of their children. These schools were sometimes taught by persons of their own color ; at other times white persons were employed as their teachers. The good effects of these early advantages, though subsequently denied them, have left indelible traces upon the negro population. It appreciates and responds quickly to all our appliances. North Carolina is among the very few States where the schools thus early in the season have increased above the highest number of last year

The enlarged plans of the assistant commissioner, General N. A. Miles, are seen in his annual report dated October 1, 1867. He says :

The importance of the educational and normal improvement of a race heretofore debarred of their benefits was early considered, and as time advanced it became almost paramount to all else. Money has been freely expended; talents brought into requisition; sacrifices made, and all have been returned with interest.

The colored people are alive to their deficiencies, and with an energy and enthusiasm unbounded, have seconded the efforts made, and are rapidly disenthralling themselves from the chains of ignorance. They will, ere long, place themselves in a position calculated to forever establish their firm foothold upon the platform of citizenship.

Sufficient progress has already been made to render the work, to a great extent, self-supporting. As each year furnishes colored persons of sufficient education to instruct others, they give themselves to the work, and thus fill up the chasms which would otherwise open as those who have preceded them pass away.

Until a recent period the bureau has looked to benevolent associations for the assistance so freely given in furnishing teachers. But now, although these societies are still engaged as earnestly in the cause as ever, yet teachers from among the masses are coming forth, and are working to the same great end.

The answer of children.—The stereotyped answer of children to the question, "What do you intend to do when you grow up to be men and women, and become educated !" has been, "I am going to be a teacher." This may appear insignificant and unmeaning to a casual observer; yet, in my opinion, it is the keynote to the fulfilment of a work conceived in the Divine mind, and is among the events which will result in Ethiopia stretching out her hands to God.

We still need assistance in continuing the work so well begun, for through the benevolent societies only can we at present fully supply the ever increasing demand.

Doubts removed.—The past school year has been one to which all can look back with great satisfaction. Doubts, fears and obstacles seemed to present themselves, but as the year advanced these gradually disappeared, and the result has exceeded the most sanguine expectations.

From the statistics it will be seen that the gain during the year ending October, 1867, has been 101 schools, 145 teachers, and 8,257 pupils; in other words, while the schools have more than doubled, the number of teachers has trebled, and that of the pupils nearly quadrupled.

The schools under the auspices of the bureau were closed for the summer, and advantage was taken of the intermission to prepare buildings and other fixtures for the winter session.

Freedmen pushing forward.—It is very gratifying to note the interest taken by the colored people themselves in pushing forward the educational work. Of late, numerous applications have been received for small sums of money to assist them in purchasing materials for school buildings, the labor being performed by their own hands. The appropriations for the current fiscal year will, in a great measure, be devoted to such cases, thus spreading over a large portion of the State facilities heretofore limited in their character.

The indifference of the white people in this State to the importance of free schools is deplorable. As far as I have been able to learn, there are but three free white schools in the State. There are many private institutions, where only those children whose parents are able to pay tuition are benefited : and the result is, that thousands of white men and women over 21 years of age cannot read and write, as will be seen by last census, which gives the number of this class at 73,566.

Education and loyalty.—A system of education where all children between the ages of 7 and 14 would be obliged to attend school would be of the greatest advantage to the people of the State, as well as a benefit to the whole country. It is my belief that, had this people been as liberally educated, and with the same advantages for general information, as is found in the northern States, they would never have been dragged into the rebellion.

Skilled labor.—Another evidence of the evil arising from this indifference to education is also seen in the absence among the white population of skilled labor in every branch of industry.

This last remark of the commissioner reveals a striking fact, viz : that the above labor is, in this State, to a large extent performed by colored men. North Carolina has never been distinguished as an agricultural State. Their slaves were valuable as fitted for high prices in the market or for some productive labor at home. They were therefore, in large numbers, made to learn the different trades; and as all labor by white men was considered dishonorable, the trades of course fell into their hands. The result is, as Mr. Langston, who lately inspected the State, remarks, that "more than one-third of the entire colored population of North Carolina are mechanics. They are nearly six to one as compared with white mechanics. The census gives less than 20,000 of the latter and more than 100,000 of the former. All the mechanical occupations are represented by them; blacksmiths, gunsmiths, wheelwrights, millwrights, machinists, carpenters, cabinet-makers, plasterers, painters, ship-builders, stone-masons, and bricklayers are found among them in large numbers. They have also many pilots and engineers. Nor are they behind any class of workmen in the skill, taste, and ability which are usually exhibited in their several trades. Of the pilots and engineers running steamboats on the different rivers of this State, many of the very best are colored men. It is said that the two most trustworthy pilots in North Carolina are freedmen, one of whom is running a steamboat on Cape Fear river, and the other across Albemarle sound and on the Chowan and Blackwater rivers. The former is paid fifteen dollars per month more than any other pilot on the river, because of his superior ability. The engineer on the boat run by this pilot is also a freedman, and is said to be one of the best in the State.

"These colored mechanics when employed command the usual wages paid others of the same calling, although in the days of slavery no colored man, according to the law, could act as master-workman upon a job, but must always be subordinate to a white man; yet the freed mechanics are now constantly taking work upon their own responsibility and doing it to the satisfaction of their employés. One of the most interesting sights which it was my good fortune to witness while in the State was the building of a steamboat on Cape Fear river by a colored ship-builder, with his gang of colored workmen."

The inspector reports in October that schools have been established in some fifty-two of the counties of the State. "Most of these schools are in good condition as to numbers, attendance, and deportment; others need special and immediate attention." I must, however, state that the sub-assistant commissioners and agents of the bureau in this State, with some very commendable exceptions, do not visit the schools or hold educational meetings among the people as they ought in compliance with your circular No. 5. They are also too indifferent to the improvement of adult freedmen. The consequence is, the freedmen remain in ignorance of what they themselves *can* and what they *ought* to do with regard to education and the aid proffered them by the government through the bureau.

The inspector goes on to say:

Educational meetings.—Educational meetings should be held throughout the State, especially where there are no schools, at which addresses to the freedmen should be made upon their importance and the necessity of building them up, as far as may be, by the use of their own means, particularly in the purchase of sites for school-houses, and giving them a full explanation with regard to the assistance which will be furnished by the government.

In many places in this State the buildings used for school purposes are very poor, being wanting in capacity as well as in such construction and arrangement as to make them convenient and desirable. This is true of Hillsboro', Fayetteville, Chapel Hill, Goldsboro', Newton, and Catawba stations, not to mention other places, and of several buildings used in Raleigh, Newberne, Morehead City, and Wilmington.

School-houses.—School-houses have been built by the bureau or some benevolent associations of the north in many of the more prominent places of the State. In Raleigh the bureau has completed a very beautiful and convenient one, with two rooms, and is erecting a second, much larger, two stories high, with four large and commodious rooms. It is also aiding in the completion of two others in the same city.

In Newbern it has completed a good one, and is building another, to be finished very soon: while in Lincolnton, Charlotte, Greensboro', Salisbury, Hillsboro', Raleigh, Goldsboro', Newberne, Morehead City, Beaufort, Wilmington, and Fayetteville, the benevolent associations, aided by the bureau, have provided, in several instances, good buildings; but in almost all of the smaller towns of the State, as well as the rural districts, there are as yet no school-houses.

The schools of this State are conducted generally in the spirit of a large Christain liberality, aiming at nothing other than the education and elevation of all children and adults who come within their influence. It would be well if no agencies in the field were influenced by sectarian considerations. The schools of the Protestant Episcopal Commission, however, bear the significant appellation of "parochial;" and their teachers are often unwilling, and in some instances forbidden, to unite with teachers employed by other organizations in forming teachers' associations. Thus, uniformity in the modes of discipline and instruction, and cordial co-operation on the part of all the teachers, are unattainable.

Teachers' associations.—I succeeded in forming three teachers' associations; one at Raleigh, another at Newbern, and a third at Wilmington. At Newbern, Miss Chapin and Miss Hicks, teachers of the Episcopal schools, permitted our meeting to be held at their home, and gave the teachers who met there a cordial reception.

I found in this State several industrial schools among the freedmen. They appeared to be for the most part composed of scholars from the other schools. Many of the day schools are very large, well classified, thoroughly disciplined, and the children making rapid progress in their studies, and all that pertains to a well-ordered school life. In this connection, the school taught by Misses S. J. Woodson and V. S. Williams, colored ladies, at Hillsboro', may be mentioned; also, the schools of Robert and Cicero Harris, colored gentlemen, at Fayetteville: the "Williston school," at Wilmington, taught by Miss Laura J. Noble, in the primary department and Miss H. W. Goodman, in the grammar department; the Episcopal school, at Newbern, taught by Mr. B. Winfield; the one taught by John Lewis, esquire, at Charlotte; the one at Greensboro', taught by Miss M. B. Bowman; the one at Raleigh, taught by Miss Graves, and the "Washburn school," at Beaufort, taught by John Scott, as principal, assisted by Miss Mary Williams and Miss S. A. Beals. These are all large and admirably conducted.

Not many night schools have been opened as yet. They will be commenced and thoroughly organized for the winter work about the middle of December.

Sabbath schools.—In all the cities of the State, in most of the smaller towns, and in many of the rural districts Sabbath schools are established and well conducted. Many of them are managed by the freedmen themselves, others only taking a helping part, while the officers, (superintendents, secretaries, treasurers, and librarians,) and not a few of their teachers, are colored persons, formerly slaves.

By the arrangements now being made for grading and classifying the schools, the progress of the children generally must be rapid and thorough.

Educational associations.—Great credit is due the educational associations generally for what they have done in this State. Especially are they entitled to our gratitude for the wisdom exhibited in the selection and appointment of most of their teachers. No less can be said than that those teachers are earnest, laborious, self-sacrificing, able, and efficient. Most of their schools make no charge for tuition. In some of them there is a charge of 25 cents per month per scholar, made to meet incidental expenses, but in no case is any child excluded by the inability of parents or friends to pay this amount. Scholars are generally expected to furnish their own books, and this they do very promptly. In some cases of extreme poverty books are lent to pupils.

Credit to white men.—It is but just that I report the existence of very much genuine earnest feeling on the part of many white men favorable to the education of the freedmen. In the neighborhood of Edenton, Chowan county, and along the eastern shore of the State, in many places, schools are being established and taught without molestation or disturbance from any quarter.

Mr. J. M. Parott, the owner of a large plantation near Kinston, has built a school-house, in which the children of his former slaves, most of whom remain with him, are regularly taught by a colored teacher of some attainments, who is actuated by an earnest interest in the elevation of his race. Children on other plantations are permitted to attend this school. It numbers 75 pupils, with an average daily attendance of 50. In this school there is a monthly charge of $1 per scholar made for tuition. It is reported that this charge is very generally and promptly paid. The utmost good feeling is said to exist among the white and colored people on this plantation.

Colonel W. R. Myers, of Charlotte, has given eight acres of good land located about one mile from the centre of the town, said to be worth $600, as a site upon which to erect the "Biddle Memorial Institute," and the dwellings of the teachers connected therewith.

Newspaper.—At Raleigh, the capital of the State, the freedmen have just established and are now issuing a very respectable weekly newspaper called "The Republican." This paper, edited and published by colored men, is gaining quite a full circulation among the people.

Benevolent societies.—Here at the capital, as in other parts of the State, there are many literary and benevolent societies, some composed of men, others of women, which are exerting a beneficial influence. The "Relief Society," of which Mrs. Robert Wyche, of Raleigh, is the president, which did so much for needy colored women during the war, and which is still caring for that class, deserves special notice.

Poor whites.—Miss Chapin's school for poor whites at Beaufort, I heard spoken of as being largely attended and earnestly and efficiently taught. The one at Wilmington, for the same class, taught by Miss A. E. Bradley, numbers 150 in its enrolment, with an average daily attendance of 125. This school is increasing rapidly, and the building used is already filled. The parents, whose children attend this school, are very poor, ignorant, and, in some cases, degraded; but many of their children are interesting and promising in appearance, and, if blessed with educational and moral influences, as they grow into man and woman hood must prove valuable members of society. It is to be hoped that these schools are but inaugurating a more general educational movement, which, under God, is to bring educa tion, with its innumerable and invaluable blessings, to more than 73,000 white persons in North Carolina, who; hitherto denied the free common school, are neither able to read nor write.

In North Carolina reports give all kinds of schools, 403; pupils, 25,631.

Of these, there are regularly reported 168 day or night schools, with 177 teachers and 10,220 pupils; 99 Sabbath schools, with 529 teachers and 8,485 pupils; 1 industrial school, with 123 pupils; 1 high or normal school, with 28 pupils. Thirty-three of these schools are graded. The freedmen own 63 of the buildings in which they are held, and pay the expenses, wholly or in part, of 90 of them. Eighty-nine of the teachers have been furnished transportation by this bureau. Two thousand four hundred and ninety-seven of the pupils pay tuition, amounting, in the last six months, to $4,776 87, or $1 91 per scholar.

The bureau has expended $13,713 96 for rental, material, and repairs of school buildings; and all parties have contributed $28,484 41 to the support of the schools.

There are 60 day and night schools, "not regularly reported," with 62 teach ers and 2,269 pupils, and 75 Sabbath schools, with 275 teachers and 4,534 pupils.

Of the 1,043 teachers employed in the above schools, 413 are white and 630 colored.

SOUTH CAROLINA.

The assistant commissioner, Brevet Major General R K. Scott, reported in October a highly satisfactory state of things He says :

In the educational department of the bureau in this State great progress has been made during the past year. There has not been a very large increase in the number of schools supported by northern societies, or in the number of pupils attending these schools; but they have been conducted with more system and greater efficiency than heretofore, and the results are entirely satisfactory. The northern teachers have evidently been selected with great care, and, in almost every instance, are well fitted for their duties.

There has been a large increase in the number of schools sustained by the freedmen them selves, though the poverty of the people has prevented them from securing the right kind of teachers. Their schools, as a consequence, are inferior, and must remain so until competent teachers can be secured.

Change of public sentiment.—During the past year a very marked change in public senti ment has taken place favorable to the establishment of schools and the education of the colored people. This change is in various ways indicated by both white and colored people.

School by a southerner—I would call attention to a school organized by and started under the direction of a southern clergyman, Rev. A. T. Porter. It is supported by various Episcopal societies of the north, and bids fair to be a successful and prosperous institution. I cannot doubt that the experiment will be an unqualified success. The number of pupils in attendance since its establishment has averaged about 300.

The city authorities, through the board of school commissioners, have furnished one of the largest and most complete school buildings in this city (Charleston) for the use of colored children. It will accommodate 1,000 pupils, and the institution, I have no doubt, when fully started, will take rank with the schools in this city now assigned exclusively to the use of whites.

Significant fact.—It is a significant fact that no schools established under the auspices of the bureau have been discontinued. The indications are that all will show, on opening this fall, a largely increased attendance and interest, and that during the coming year, as in the past, they will be found among the most potent and invaluable aids in the reconstruction of the government, and the establishment of harmony among all classes in the community.

No great result can be expected from schools not organized by some society, or under the control of the bureau; yet, as preparing the way for a common school system, they are as far as possible encouraged.

At the "Ridge" a Sunday school has been started by Mr. J. M. Morris, which numbers about 100 scholars.

Columbia.—The new school building in Columbia having been completed, the schools opened with a competent corps of teachers the second week in October. Although not yet fully organized, some 600 scholars have presented themselves, and are graded into regular classes. Great success is anticipated for schools in that city.

Edisto.—In all their reverses a large number of freedmen on Edisto island have not forgotten the education of their children. In some places it is being carried on by a very commendable system; children of 10 to 14 years are taught by young men (white) in the evenings, and for this the children labor as many hours next day as they were under tuition the previous evening.

The State superintendent, Mr. Reuben Tomlinson, reports in October as follows :

There are 23 school-houses in the State which have been built by the colored people with the aid of northern societies and this bureau. The school-house at Columbia, alluded to in the report of July 1, 1867, is now completed, and in a few days will have within its walls a large and successful school.

The normal school building in this city (Charleston) is progressing rapidly, and will doubtless be ready for use on the 1st of December.

The total amount expended by the bureau in this State for school purposes, for the year ending October 1, is $33,003 06. A few small items unreported would increase this amount slightly.

The school commissioners of this city have opened one of the public school-houses for colored children, and, so far as the city is concerned, it is probable there will be good school accommodations for all the children during the term now opening.

Country districts —I have spent the greater part of the past two months in travelling through the country districts, and have found the desire for schools intense and universal. After the crops are in the markets the people will be able to help themselves to educational privileges.

The unhealthiness of the sea islands this season will delay the opening of the schools in that part of the State until November 1. The other schools will all be in operation by the second week of this month. The indications are of a very successful year.

Crude religious instruction.—Proper religious instruction is sorely needed for the temporal as well as spiritual guidance of the people. Such clergymen as they have among them are mainly ignorant, and although teaching both by precept and example, the former is limited and crude, while oftentimes the latter is productive of a want of that confidence and love which a people should have for their religious instruction.

We call the special attention of the publishing societies to the following :

The need of proper religious books is felt, and when the ardent desire of the young to read books of this class is taken into consideration, no means more likely to be productive of good results could be devised than a copious distribution of elementary works of a religious character.

The want of missionaries capable of teaching the people is also felt, more particularly in the neighborhood of the rice swamps. I would respectfully suggest that associations sending out missionaries have here in South Carolina a field for their resources which would compensate them better than many other localities.

In addition to the schools reported, there are in the city of Charleston two schools for colored children ; one sustained by the board of school commissioners, numbering about 400 pupils, and one sustained by the Methodist Freedmen's Association, numbering about 150 pupils.

Monthly contribution.—In some localities a rigid enforcement of the rule adopted by the northern societies, and recommended by this bureau, requiring a monthly contribution from the pupils, has had the effect of diminishing the numbers attending the schools. But this regulation will, in the end, prove beneficial, and even now no serious injury is done to the schools by its enforcement.

It is reported from the northern part of the State that there is an increasing desire on the part of the freedmen to have schools established. Officers of the bureau encourage every effort of this kind, but for want of funds they cannot accomplish much.

There are many places (says the sub-assistant commissioner at Aiken) where it is desirable and practicable to establish schools, but where northern teachers could not be sent, though native teachers might be employed.

Small grants of land, made by the aid societies, would be the means of effecting great good if given to schools in all these parts.

In his report for December the State superintendent says :

My report shows no increase in the number of scholars or pupils as compared with this time a year ago. This is to be regretted, but is unavoidable, for the reason that the northern societies are unable to extend their work, and the people of the State, so far as money is concerned, are poorer than they were a year ago.

Summary.—Schools of all kinds in South Carolina, 201; pupils, 21,531.

Forty-five of these are day or night schools, with an enrolment of 6,743 pupils and 119 teachers; 31 Sabbath schools, with 2,788 pupils; and 2 high or normal schools, with 500 pupils. Twenty of these schools are graded into primary, intermediate, and grammar.

Of the schools "within the knowledge of the superintendent, not regularly reported," 55 are day or night schools, with 65 teachers and 5,000 pupils; and 70 Sabbath schools, with 180 teachers and 7,000 pupils.

Four of the school buildings are owned by the freedmen themselves, and they sustain, wholly or in part, 30 of the above schools.

The bureau has expended for material, rents, and repairs of school buildings in this State, $2,062 67, and furnished transportation to 26 teachers.

In support of the above schools for the six months, by all parties, the amount has reached $17,000.

There has been paid, by 335 of the pupils in the day and night schools, $3,467 65 for tuition, or an average of $10 35 per scholar.

The whole number of teachers reported is 364; white 154, colored 210.

The average attendance on the enrolment in the day and night schools has been a fraction over 79 per cent.

GEORGIA.

There is a very good local organization of schools in this State, of which we have previously spoken, and which we commend as a model. Thus far the people seem capable of managing it successfully.

General C. C. Sibley, the assistant commissioner, in his report speaks of it as a body of great influence :

The educational association organized in this State has now several subordinate associations supporting schools. More than half the number of the State board of this association are members of the constitutional convention.

A meeting of the board will be called when the convention reassembles, and in connection with the committee of the convention a suitable provision for public schools will be prepared for insertion in the constitution, or at least proposed to the convention, by whom it will be, very probably, adopted.

Brevet Brigadier General F. D. Sewall, bureau inspector, reports from Georgia as follows :

Generally, matters are in a very satisfactory condition in this State. In the upper counties the freedmen are doing well, but the reports from the southern part of the State indicate some lawlessness, resulting from the unsettled condition of business affairs.

Mr. E. A. Ware, superintendent of education for this State, is prosecuting the educational work vigorously and with the most practical results.

The general inspector of schools reports the educational work here as "very thoroughly and successfully done." The organization of the State for educational purposes is complete, the people are accessible, and the schools well attended.

Educational association.—The Georgia Educational Association deserves special notice. It is the purpose of this organization

To associate the efforts of the people, the prominent educators in the State, the agents of northern societies, and such officers of the government as are authorized to aid in the work, and to unite them in such a manner as shall exclude any subject at all likely to divide their efforts or divert them from their one great and desirable object. To secure this end subordinate associations are established as far as practicable. By this means a thorough union is formed and a prompt and constant communication with the parent society is had. Connected with the State association is a State board of education, which, as to its character and duties, is a general executive committee. This board, in an address of June 15, 1867, expresses a desire to co-operate with the agents of all societies and associations that propose to labor in this State; and, with the agents of the bureau, cordially invites them to aid in the organization of these associations, and to give advice and supervision so far as may be in their power.

The board hopes to meet such a response from the people as shall, under the blessing of Providence, result in much present good, and laying deep and permanently the foundation of a system of public instruction which shall, in time, place an education within the reach of all the citizens of Georgia.

Great good has already been accomplished by this association. The persons, white and colored, interested in the education of the people, have been brought together and made acquainted with each other's plans, purposes, and views. Quite considerable sums of money have been raised to aid in the general and local work, and many schools established, which, without this organization, could not have been commenced.

This organization, too, has in a very important sense, in not a few communities, developed and stimulated the self-reliant spirit of the freed people. As showing this, we now find that in each of the ten sub-districts of Georgia there is at least one school, and in one or two of them there are not less than twenty.

The classification, grading, and discipline of the schools in Georgia are for the most part satisfactory. The attendance is good, being generally prompt and regular. Little tardiness is mentioned. The progress of the children in their studies and deportment is, all things considered, very fair. The text books used generally are the national series. This is in accordance with special order by the superintendent of education. The register used is the one furnished by the bureau.

The Sabbath schools number 60, with an attendance of 7,000. The superintendents are for the most part colored men, and many of the teachers are colored persons also. Their management is generally good. I found no school in this State which deserves the name of normal. Some of the scholars, in several of the schools, are getting on quite well with their studies, but none of them are sufficiently advanced to begin to give attention to the different theories and methods of *imparting* instruction. The most advanced have not yet mastered the ordinary books of grammar, arithmetic, geography, reading, and writing.

What the freedmen have done by way of raising funds to be used for repairing or building school-houses, or in buying land for school purposes, cannot be given with exactness. They furnish 25 churches for which no rent is charged. Some of their schools they support entirely, employing teachers, paying the rents, and providing for all incidental expenses.

In all of the schools there is a tuition charged of from 25 cents to $1 per month per scholar. The following associations patronize schools in this State: The American Missionary Association; this association has charge of and supports 70 schools. Union Educational Society; this society has charge of and supports one school. The New England Branch F. U. Commission, has charge of and supports seven schools. The National Theological Institute and University for Colored Ministers and Teachers, has charge of and supports one school. The Freedmen's Aid Society of the Methodist Church, supports eight schools.

School buildings.—The bureau has erected three new school-houses; one at Athens, another at Americus, and a third at Savannah. Two good and substantial buildings have been erected in part by the bureau, at Atlanta. Twenty-nine buildings, 19 of which are churches, have been repaired by the bureau. It has now in process of erection three new buildings; one at Macon, another at Griffin, and the other at Brunswick. These are all near y finished, and will be dedicated in a few weeks. There are six military buildings us d for schools.

One of the finest gatherings of children that I have had the pleasure of addressing in the south was one held on the 11th of last month, in the chapel of "Storr's school," in Atlanta, and composed of the scholars of that school only. The children demeaned themselves with great propriety.

It was my good fortune, while in Macon, to see in one gathering, at the Methodist church, all the children of the several schools. This gathering numbered, with their teachers, 525 persons. On the following Sabbath I saw all the Sabbath schools of the city, in their usual monthly Sabbath school concert, as they gathered in the Baptist church. This gathering numbered 868, and was one of the most interesting of the sort I ever saw. There were not a few aged black men and women among those who made recitations of Scripture texts, and as the sacred words came from their untutored memories and trembling lips, they sank with a new power upon the souls of many present, who, from the depths of grateful hearts whispered the ejaculation, "Thank God."

In connection with these schools a very fine and flourishing temperance organization of the "vanguard of freedom," known as the "Howard Division," has been organized.

Former times.—As indicating the education of former times, we give the following fact: One of the teachers in Savannah, a colored lady, Miss Deveaux, who teaches a private school, has been teaching in the same building, and in the same room in which she now teaches, for the last 33 years. Although quite advanced in life, she labors with earnestness and zeal. It is especially interesting to hear her relate how her work was carried on in secret, eluding, for more than a quarter of a century the most constant and lynx-eyed vigilance of the slave-holders of her native city. She has been instrumental, under God, of aiding in the education of many colored persons, who, scattered here and there through the south, are now able to contribute somewhat towards the general elevation of the newly-emancipated race. Her school is the one in which are now found the children of the better class of the colored people of Savannah. This is just as one might expect, for she is well and favorably known among them.

The largest and most interesting night school I have seen is that held in the Beach Institute, under the charge of Mr. O. W. Dimick. On the evening of the 18th of last month this school numbered 208. Too great praise cannot be awarded Mr. Dimick, for the interesting and efficient manner in which the schools of this Institute are conducted. This building, in which eight schools are kept, and which was erected by the bureau, is, in its construction and its furniture, a model.

One hundred schools wanted.—All over this State there is an intelligent feeling on the part of the freedmen in favor of schools; and the demand for them is growing in all directions. More than a hundred could be organized and opened at once, were the means at hand. The sentiment of the white people generally seems not to be unfavorable to the education of the colored people.

Poor whites.—At Atlanta there are two schools for poor whites, supported by the Pennsylvania and New Jersey Union Commission. They number in their enrolment 255 pupils, with an average attendance of 180.

The statistical returns of this State give the aggregate number of all kinds of schools 173; pupils, 12,428. These schools are taught by 237 teachers—151 white and 86 colored—78 of whom have been furnished transportation by this bureau.

Of the above schools regularly reported, 96 are day or night, with 125 teachers and 6,088 pupils; 54 Sabbath, with 100 teachers and 5,410 pupils; 1 industrial, with 30 pupils, and 3 high or normal, with 100 pupils. Those "within the knowledge of the superintendent" are 12 day or night schools, with 12 teachers and 305 pupils, and 10 Sabbath schools, with 595 pupils.

Of the whole number of schools reported, 91 are sustained, wholly or in part, by the freedmen themselves, and they own 27 of the buildings in which schools are held.

A tuition fee, amounting in the aggregate to $1,700, has been paid by 1,373 of the pupils in the day and night schools. The average attendance has been 4,493, or over 73 per cent.

FLORIDA.

In the district of Florida the superintendence has been vigorous, with excellent plans for an increase of schools and for their local support. The whole number of schools of all descriptions at the present time, as reported, is 125, with 5,592 pupils. This is a large increase over the highest numbers reported at any time during the last year.

Of the above, 67 are day or night schools, with 56 teachers and 3,085 pupils; 27 Sabbath schools, with 1,046 pupils, and 2 industrial schools.

Those "not regularly reported" are 23 day or night schools, with 35 teachers and 764 pupils, and 6 Sabbath schools, with 88 teachers and 697 pupils.

Eight of the regularly reported day schools are graded, viz: primary, intermediate, and grammar.

Of the 179 teachers employed, 78 are white and 101 colored. Transportation has been furnished to 16 of these by this bureau. There are 40 white pupils in daily attendance. Seven of the day or night schools are held in buildings owned by the freedmen, and 16 are sustained wholly or in part by them. Tuition to the amount of $250 has been paid by 246 pupils.

General J. T. Sprague, the assistant commissioner, reports in September:

Effect of schools.—Soon as it can be determined what the result of the crop will be, a much larger amount of land will be entered under the homestead bill than heretofore. The industry of freedmen, judiciously caring for themselves, together with a personal pride in all that relates to his family, have been apparent this season far more than at any former period, and, if continued, will encourage the friends of the race in the belief that their labor can be used to great advantage. Florida is an apt illustration of this remark, and, as I think, churches and schools have been the principal cause.

Remarkable zeal.—In October the assistant commissioner says:

The freedmen have everywhere displayed remarkable zeal and self-denial in all things pertaining to education, in several instances constructing school-houses at their own expense, unaided from any source, and afterwards contributing from their limited funds for the support of a teacher. Where this spirit is manifested I have avoided interfering, deeming it better policy to encourage self-dependence in this as in all other matters relating to these people.

There has been expended in Florida for construction, rental, and repairs of school-buildings and asylums during the year $6,410 55.

School societies.—The system of organizing school societies over the State, under the direction of sub-assistant commissioners, is proving of great advantage. Land is purchased by contribution, and, upon the title being secured to the society, the officer of the sub-district is charged with constructing the school-building upon plans and estimates furnished him. In this manner numbers of school-houses are now in process of construction through the State.

There is great want of a larger number of competent teachers, many colored teachers in the interior being quite incompetent. No better, however, can be found in the State who are willing to teach for the doubtful compensation received.

It is my intention to dot the State with small buildings in the vicinity of large plantations, thus permitting the attendance of all the children without requiring a walk of more than one or two miles.

Planters co-operate—The owners of plantations enter into this plan most cordially, and readily furnish land enough upon which to place the buildings, while the labor is mainly contributed by the freedmen in sawing timber and raising the buildings. The bureau is to furnish windows, doors, nails, and seasoned lumber. In this manner the school fund will be most usefully and economically applied, while a comfortable building will be within reach of all the families interested, which may be used both as school-house and church.

It is evident from the above statement that Florida will be among the first of the southern States to establish and sustain a public school system for all children.

ALABAMA.

In Alabama we have to report total schools, 96; pupils, 7,100.

Of these 70 are day or night schools, with 83 teachers and 4,435 pupils; and 26 Sabbath schools, with 2,665 pupils.

The freedmen sustain wholly or in part nine of the above schools, and six of the buildings are owned by themselves.

A tuition fee is paid by 303 of the pupils attending the day or night schools. The average attendance has been 3,200, or 72 per cent. of the whole enrolment.

Of the above pupils 705 are in alphabet, 2,611 spell and read easy lessons, 1,119 are advanced readers, 457 in geography, 796 in arithmetic, and 91 in the higher branches.

Of the teachers employed 68 are white and 15 colored.

General Wager Swayne, the assistant commissioner, in his report for October, remarks that preparation is making to erect large buildings for schools of a high order at Mobile, Montgomery and Selma, and others are in contemplation. The title has in every case been vested in a board of suitable trustees, with proper guarantee against a failure of the trust.

At points less central, and on plantations, many rude school-rooms have been put up, and these the bureau has assisted with school furniture. Applications for help in all ways have steadily increased throughout the year, the demand being greater than could be supplied.

Two small buildings have been destroyed by incendiarism, and some individual lawlessness has been encountered; but the severe hostility at first so general has now disappeared.

Important aid has been received from missionary associations of the north.

Sabbath schools and Bibles.—It is noteworthy that the voluntary labor of the teachers has imparted Sabbath school instruction to 8,000 pupils, and that, through the office of the school superintendent, more than 5,000 Bibles, and Testaments kindly donated for the purpose by the American Bible Society, have been distributed among the freedmen, most of whom for the first time in their lives thus came into possession of the word of God.

The average cost of these schools to the government has been 61¼ cents per month for each scholar in actual daily attendance.

The entire expenditure for school purposes has been $45,237 55. The increased ability of parents of the pupils to sustain schools warrants an attempt to make them wholly self-supporting.

Judicious organization.—The general school inspector says in the report of a late tour through this State:

My observation leads me to the conclusion that the only thing now needed in Alabama to enlarge the number of schools and increase by thousands the number of those attending, is a thorough and judicious organization of the work and a wise and earnest instruction of the freedmen as to their duty and interest in the premises.

Favorable indications.—I found no opposition on the part of the better and influential class of white people to the education of the freedmen, and no other than a manly purpose on the part of the freedmen themselves to do all in their power to help themselves in this direction. They are not only willing to send their children to the schools, but wherever able are willing to aid financially in supporting them.

In this connection I cannot pass over the fact that, at Mount Moriah, six miles from Montgomery, lives a colored man by the name of Edward Moore, who has built a log school-house at his own expense and on his own land, and now teaches a school therein which numbers 52 pupils, with an average attendance of 40. This school is entirely supported by the freedmen.

Nor can I pass in silence the fact that at Selma there lives a freedman by the name of B. S. Turner, one of the firm of Turner & Co., who is an energetic and thrifty business man, and who has already accumulated a handsome property. Mr. Turner is not only interested in his own education but in that of the children of his friends and neighbors. His exact words to me were: "Let us educate: let us make sacrifices to educate ourselves; in this matter let us help those of us who are unable to help themselves." In the accumulation of property, and as to the purpose and sentiment contained in the above words, he is a representative man among the freedmen.

Blue College building.—In Mobile a large fine brick structure, located about one mile and a half out Government street, and known as the Blue College building, has been, through the aid of the bureau, and from private sources, purchased by the American Missionary Association. It is proposed, after making certain repairs upon this building, to put all their schools at Mobile into it. This building is one of great capacity, and will soon be in good condition for use. Its location, too, is faultless, and the colored people of all classes, as well as their friends, appreciate this magnificent gift. The furniture in this building is very good, being durable and of the most approved modern make. It has also a complete set of philosophical and chemical apparatus, provided by the school commissioners of the city. The school is now called the Emerson School, in honor of Mr. Emerson, of Rockford, Illinois, who contributed quite liberally toward its establishment.

It is expected that the impulse given to the educational work in this city, in the purchase of this building, and the removal of the schools thereto, as well as their reorganization under competent teachers, will very soon swell the numbers in attendance to over one thousand.

Montgomery.—In Montgomery I found seven schools, six in charge of the American Missionary Association, under a corps of able and efficient teachers, and one taught by Mr. William M. Lottin, a white man of southern birth and education. The latter school is a private one. It numbers 150 pupils, with an average attendance of 110. Connected with this is a night school which numbers 40 scholars.

The attendance upon the schools of this city is too small, being only about 489. This number, however, is for the most part prompt and quite regular.

There are two Sabbath schools in Montgomery, one held in the Baptist and the other in the Zion Methodist church, colored. These are interesting and flourishing schools, and number about 250 scholars each. The superintendents are both colored men, and are earnest and efficient. The teachers are also mainly colored persons. Teachers of the day schools all aid in the management and general conduct of these Sabbath schools.

A beautiful site for a school-house has already been purchased by the colored people of Montgomery, and as soon as the building is erected thereon a new impulse will be given to the educational work. It is to be hoped that the building will be erected without further delay.

Selma.—At Selma there are four day schools. One is in charge of the session of the Presbyterian church of Selma (white,) and is taught by Rev. J. A. Walker, assisted by his wife. This school was opened May 1, 1867. For the first month it averaged only 15 pupils; the second month, 30; and the third, 50. It has grown steadily in numbers until it now enrolls about 60 scholars.

The children in the schools of Selma are pursuing the common English branches, and are doing quite well in their studies, but are not well graded nor classified. There is a great need of a good school-house at this place. A very eligible site has been purchased for such building, and an appropriation of some $4,000 has been made by the bureau for its erection.

Individual effort.—W. M. Buckley, esq., the owner of a plantation some forty miles from Montgomery, in Lowndes county, has built a good frame school-house for the accommodation of the freedmen employed by him, as well as others of that class living in the neighborhood. The bureau furnished sixty dollars' worth of materials for this building. This school now numbers 60 pupils, with an average attendance of 50. Connected with it is a Sabbath school of 80 persons. Mr. Buckley is a northern man. He informed me, however, that there are not a few white men of southern birth in his particular neighborhood whose sentiments with regard to the education of the former slaves are now favorable and improving constantly.

Thus much I have said about particular places. I might speak of others in the same manner; but your attention should be called to the work in its broader features. In this State there are sixty-two counties. These constitute ten sub-districts under the bureau.

From my observation two things are apparent: first, a great many of these counties, and some especially densely populated by the freed people, are wholly without schools; and secondly, exclusive of the scholars attending night and Sabbath schools, there is only a small portion of the children of freedmen attending school in any of these counties.

Buildings and teachers.—The buildings furnished by the bureau for school purposes are generally good; in a few instances they are poor. The number owned by the government is ten. Preparations are being made for the erection of several others.

Of the teachers engaged in the schools, as far as my observation goes, it is but just to say that they are generally earnest, laborious and efficient. The discipline of the schools is, in the main, good, and the instruction in many accurate and thorough.

MISSISSIPPI.

From the assistant commissioner of this State, Brevet Major General A. C. Gillem, we learn that measures are in progress for thorough reorganization of the school system for the fall and winter sessions.

Large numbers of applications are being made for teachers on plantations. They come from planters, who agree to furnish buildings; the freedmen agreeing to pay tuition.

These schools deserve, and are receiving every encouragement.

The disposition of the whites towards the freed people is, as a general thing, very satisfactory. Nevertheless, there does not appear in any class a very general confidence in the capability of the negro to attain a high degree of civilization. The whites are willing to accord to him that justice and aid which may be of use in his sphere, or which may be granted by a superior to an inferior race, but do not seem to recognize his claims as due from man to man. They regard the colored race as inferiors by nature, and believe that no legislation or philanthropy can elevate them from the state in which they consider nature has placed them.

In his annual report, the assistant commissioner says:

'The efficiency of the schools in the principal cities and towns has been impaired for want of being properly graded, particularly in those places where schools have been in operation since the close of the war. The chief obstacle, however, has been the want of proper buildings in which to conduct graded schools. There have been but two of that class in the State during the past year, one at Vicksburg, and the other at Columbus. The former has been conducted under the auspices of the United Presbyterians, with a corps of experienced teachers. This school has by its success demonstrated the necessity as well as the utility of proper organization.

But few cases of open hostility or violence have been reported in many months.

The report of the superintendent of education, Captain H. R. Pease, for November, gives an encouraging view. He says:

It affords me pleasure to be able to report an increase of upwards of 1,000 pupils during this month.

I have made arrangements for opening a number of new schools at points where none have hitherto existed.

The unsettled condition of the freedmen in consequence of the failure of the cotton crop will present, and indeed has already presented an obstacle in carrying out my plan of organizing school societies on the plantations.

Planters are undecided whether they will carry on their plantations at all next year or not, and therefore the freedmen are unprepared to take any definite action in establishing schools.

School lands.—In relation to the subject of school lands of this State, I have been unable to arrive at anything definite as yet. It appears to be a very complicated matter. The records for the past six years, and particularly during the war, are incomplete. But there is evidently a large amount of money, due the school fund from the sale and rental of these public lands, unpaid.

Special inspection.—The plan of requiring a special inspection and report from the sub-assistant commissioners is the only practicable method by which the educational work for this State can be fairly exhibited, and thereby enable us to arrange in detail the business of the department for the ensuing year.

3 F S

The reports indicate that these inspections have, with but few exceptions, been thoroughly made. They are replete with evidence that the concomitants of slavery still remain, and that the bureau, or some similar institution to act as a protector and conservator for the freedmen, is absolutely necessary. Should the bureau be withdrawn, the freedmen, in my opinion, would suffer for some time to come, even under the most favorable State government which could, in that case, be reasonably expected.

The deep-seated prejudices of caste, and the innate disposition of the former slave owners to degrade labor and withhold the elevating influence of education from the masses, white and colored, will continue to operate against the faithful and impartial execution of the most liberal, humane, and equitable laws.

Time and stern necessity will no doubt materially modify existing prejudices, and, indeed, there seems to be a growing disposition on the part of many to accept the situation as a necessity and adapt themselves to it.

Poverty.—In many portions of the State, owing to failure of the crop, the freedmen will be utterly unable to contribute towards supporting schools. Still, I am happy to be able to state that from present indications we shall materially increase the educational work in this State for the ensuing year.

There will, probably, be a small falling off in the number of teachers and schools supported by northern benevolent associations this year, but the increased facilities for supporting plantation schools and schools supported by the freedmen, will more than make up the deficiency.

School society.—I have formed a school society for freedmen in the city of Vicksburg. They propose to build a large house, combining with it a public hall. There is now subscribed over two thousand dollars, and the prospect is favorable for raising two thousand more in a few weeks.

The following extracts are from the reports of the several sub-districts of the State:

Meridian Sub-district.—On or before the 1st day of November next the sub-assistant commissioner will endeavor to put in operation several smaller schools on plantations in the sub-district, and will in every possible way exert his utmost influence in advancing the educational interests of the freedmen under his charge.

Corinth Sub-district.—I find that little interest in the subject of education is manifested in this sub-district. The freedmen are generally too poor to render any assistance, and the whites are disposed to discourage rather than aid in the education of the freedmen.

Oxford Sub-district.—I have not been able to ascertain upon what plantations schools can be established to advantage, from the fact that the landholders are almost universally opposed to free schools. A Mr. Dorum started a school about twelve miles from this place and it was immediately burned.

East Pascagoula Sub-district.—This district is very sparsely inhabited, and although there are about two thousand colored people living in it, they are scattered about so extensively, and so inaccessible in consequence of rivers, bayous and swamps, as to render the maintenance of schools extremely doubtful.

Aberdeen Sub-district.—The disposition of the freedmen is, as elsewhere, universally in favor of education. The whites accept it as necessary to keep their laborers in good humor, with a desire to keep the management in their own hands.

Macon Sub-district.—The freedmen express a willingness to pay a dollar a month tuition. There are many not able to do so on account of the falling off of the cotton crop and prices from the calculation made two months ago.

Woodville Sub-district.—No help can be expected from the citizens, as very little interest is manifested in regard to the welfare of the freedmen. Planters have also refused, with but one or two exceptions, to aid them.

Columbus Sub-district.—Educational matters do not prosper very well in the rural districts of this county. A prejudice exists against educating the freedmen, which is difficult to overcome. Planters seem deaf to argument, and no better illustration can be given than the quotation from Goldsmith's Deserted Village: "E'en though vanquished he could argue still." There is, however, one exception which really does one good to write of. I refer to the school taught by Miss Blackman, of Philadelphia, Pennsylvania, on the plantation of Dr. Tucker, near Okolona.

De Kalb Sub-district.—I have learned that while it is a fact the freedmen desire to take up homesteads or government lands in the county, which can be had without cost, yet they choose to purchase old, wornout fields, at several dollars per acre, provided they can be near where our schools are in progress.

Panola Sub-district.—Many of the planters are seeing the necessity of educating the negroes for their own protection and benefit. In some parts of this county they are advancing quite rapidly; in others no effort is being made for the colored race.

Tupelo Sub-district.—I have found no opposition from any citizens towards the organization of schools for freedmen during my tour of inspection. All whom I have conversed with upon the subject favor the enterprise and consider it an important step towards securing the confidence and contentment of the freedmen.

Louisville Sub district.—Since the 1st of October, 1867, I visited most of the towns and principal plantations in my charge. I learned that there was not a school in the sub-district. One had been established, but the opposition of certain citizens at Louisville caused it to be a failure. They commenced in the same way with me, but I told them in an address at Louisville that their opposition would be useless, for I was determined to succeed if it took a garrison of United States soldiers to protect me.

Hernando Sub-district.—The freedmen are generally very anxious to have opportunities offered them to become educated and to send their children to school. Little assistance can be expected from the whites.

If a few teachers could be sent here and make a start in some of the most important towns it would not be long before a dozen schools would be flourishing in this district.

Raleigh Sub-district.—The white population are favorably inclined to the education of the colored people. In this vicinity they are quite orderly and well disposed. Similar feelings of kindness prevail at other localities. In some, however, those who are willing to establish plantation schools are not ready to face the prevailing prejudice.

Lauderdale Sub-district.—Upon careful inspection I find that the condition of the freed people in this district, in an educational point of view, is not good. I cannot say the cause is attributable to any lack of zeal on their part, for as a general thing they exhibit much anxiety in the matter, and when schools are accessible they patronize them as far as in their power; but it is to be accounted for in the great scarcity of competent teachers who are of the proper material.

Williamsburg Sub-district.—There seems to be a disposition on the part of most of the planters in this district to aid as far as possible in establishing schools for freedmen.

Greenville Sub-district.—The colored people here, with very few exceptions, are totally destitute of education: the exceptions are persons who, at most, read and write indifferently. Hardly three in a thousand can write their own names.

Everywhere I have found a great want of suitable books, and in most places there are none at all. The Sabbath schools, which would otherwise be well attended, are especially deficient in this particular.

Goodman Sub-district.—We want here good teachers who have a heart in their work. To such the greatest opportunity is now open. School-houses and scholars can easily be found, but good practical teachers are not to be had. The gentlemen whose plantations I have visited are anxious to see schools started, and say that they will help the undertaking. But the recent so-called reaction in the north is having a bad effect. Men who three months ago would do much will now do nothing. They are afraid of public opinion.

McNutt Sub-district.—Efforts are in progress to establish schools for freed people in the most central and populous places. In each case a satisfactory attendance of children and adults may be depended on.

Charleston Sub-district.—As near as I can now ascertain there are about 1,500 children in this district between the ages of five and twenty. Of this number about one-third could conveniently attend schools.

Intelligent citizens of this county are not only opposed to schools for freedmen, but entertain the idea that the colored race cannot be practically educated.

Holly Springs Sub-district.—I will do all in my power to establish schools throughout this county.

Philadelphia Sub-district.—There is little or no inducement to establish schools in this district. I found but one plantation where a small school could be organized. About twenty pupils could be induced to attend school if one were organized.

These sub-district reports give in detail a very clear and full view of our work, present and prospective, throughout the whole State.

The largest total number of schools of all kinds and pupils reported from Mississippi since July 1 is, schools, 132; pupils, 7,727.

Of the above 76 are day or night schools, with 75 teachers and 3,896 pupils, and 42 Sabbath schools, with 2,845 pupils. One high or normal school, with 127 pupils, is included in the day schools.

"Within the knowledge of the superintendent," there are 10 day or night, with 12 teachers and 477 pupils, and 4 Sabbath, with 46 teachers and 509 pupils.

Amount of tuition paid by 906 of the pupils in the day and night schools is $1,692 86, or a fraction over $1 86 per scholar.

Of the above schools 54 are sustained wholly or in part by the freedmen, who own also 12 of the buildings in which they are taught.

These schools are under the instruction of 133 teachers, 58 white and 75 colored.

The expenditure by the bureau for rents and repairs and material for school buildings for the last six months has been $1,060 51, and the amount expended by all parties $4,809 33.

LOUISIANA.

In Louisiana less has been done by the northern educational associations for the schools of freedmen than in any other State. The work is carried on through local efforts of the freedmen themselves or by the general government through the bureau. In the earlier period of their existence, the schools were sustained from a general tax, imposed by military authority. The consequence of such miscellaneous support has been great fluctuation in their prosperity, local causes having a controlling and immediate effect, either to depress or encourage.

The great riot had disastrous results, blasting, for a time, the best hopes of both the freedmen and their friends. Local political excitements, in which colored men became interested, were also adverse to the quiet interests of education. Still, the schools have been kept alive, and are making commendable progress, their numbers being greater for the last three months than in the corresponding period of last year.

From the statistical reports we find the whole number of all kinds of schools, with pupils in attendance thereon, as follows : schools, 392 ; pupils, 15,803.

Of the above, 218 are day and night schools, with 191 teachers and 7,191 pupils, and 86 Sabbath schools, with 93 teachers and 4,319 pupils. There is one normal school, with 132 pupils. Besides these, 63 day or night schools, with 81 teachers and 2,226 pupils, and 25 Sabbath schools, with 99 teachers and 2,067 pupils, are reported as "within the knowledge of the superintendent."

Nineteen of the day schools are divided into three grades, viz : primary, intermediate, and grammar.

Of the whole number of pupils reported, 1,439 are in the alphabet, 2,926 spell and read easy lessons, 1,993 are in advanced readers, 1,479 are in geography, 2,009 in arithmetic, 2,619 in writing, and 274 are in the higher branches.

Attendance in the day and night schools has averaged 6,156, or 85 per cent.

A tuition fee, amounting in the aggregate to $28,943 10, has been paid by 5,096 of the pupils in the day or night schools, averaging about $5 68 per scholar.

The freedmen themselves own 17 of the school buildings, and sustain, wholly or in part, 198 of the above schools. Of the 464 teachers employed in these schools, 193 are white and 271 colored.

The amount expended by the bureau for rents, repairs, and material for school buildings has been $3,694 55, while all parties have expended $32,637 65 in support of the schools.

The assistant commissioner, General J. A. Mower, reports in October that—

During the past year the freedmen's schools throughout the State have been supported mainly by the colored people themselves, the bureau furnishing the buildings and school furniture.

Schools and labor.—At the beginning of the year both planters and freedmen showed a great interest in having schools established. Planters could not succeed in cultivating crops without the freedmen : hence, they were necessitated to give them the advantages for acquiring an education.

Applications have been received from almost all the parish agents throughout the State asking that teachers be furnished. The majority of these applications were for colored teachers, on account of boarding accommodations, which could not generally be procured among the whites. Those employed were first examined at the office of the superintendent at these headquarters, and, if found competent, transportation was furnished them to the points where their services were required.

Tuition.—With two exceptions, the schools throughout the interior of this State have been supported by the tuition and five per cent. systems. In the cities and country towns pupils pay from $1 to $1 50 for their monthly tuition.

New Orleans.—In the city of New Orleans, notwithstanding many obstacles, schools have progressed rapidly, some of them being superior to the public white schools. The normal school will soon be able to furnish a part of the colored teachers required in this State.

Since July last, two free schools have been in progress in the city. The school board has begun examining teachers, and is preparing to open schools for colored children.

Fear of yellow fever caused a decrease of attendance in the city and some other parts of the State.

The parishes.—In the parishes throughout the interior, where the crops escaped destruction, new schools have been opened, and the average number of pupils greatly exceeds that of last year. School-houses and churches have been repaired by the bureau, thereby assisting the freedmen in the establishment of their schools. Where a church has been repaired by the bureau the educational department has had the use of the same free of rent.

With one exception, the amount expended for the repair of any one building has not exceeded the sum of $50. The total amount thus expended since October, 1866, is $908 50.

Schools self-supporting.—The freedmen have done all in their power to support the schools established for their benefit, and have seconded, with hearty co-operation, every effort made by the bureau to improve their condition. Depending entirely upon their labor for support, which, through failure of the crops, has brought little or no remuneration, it is worthy of remark that the desire and determination to educate their children have not decreased in the slightest. They regard education as all-important to secure the benefits extended through the elective franchise.

The parish of Assumption has a school taught by a colored man, and supported entirely by the freedmen.

The prospects of the freedmen are flattering. Their new status under the privileges guaranteed by acts of Congress is satisfactory to all loyal men throughout the State. They manifest much interest in availing themselves of the rights given by these laws. The numerous predictions that excesses would speedily follow their enfranchisement have been falsified by subsequent developments.

Expectations exceeded.—As a race just released from the most degrading system of slavery that ever disgraced any nation, it is a truth supported by the most incontrovertible proofs, that their progress has far exceeded the highest expectations. Subject to unrelenting persecutions by the many around them, they have shown a degree of forbearance truly commendable, rarely taking into their own hands the means of redress.

The freed people of Louisiana have been subjected to severe tests, but have always proven themselves equal to the emergency, and they are now, as they have been since their liberation, the loyal and unwavering supporters of that government which so beneficently secured to them this freedom.

Suffering.—The superintendent reports for December that the schools in this State have suffered from failure of the crops, leaving the freedmen destitute of funds to support teachers. In several instances teachers have not received more than eight or ten dollars for their whole month's labor.

In many localities planters who employed freedmen for wages during the past year have not the means to pay or even feed their laborers, and hence the latter, although willing and anxious to keep their children in school, cannot even obtain the bare necessaries of life.

Those also who have been at work for a share of the crop are left homeless, and entirely destitute of means for their subsistence, and cannot in any way support schools for their children until engaged for the next year by those who can pay monthly wages. Very many will not be able to pay a dollar for school purposes before next June or July. I am pained, therefore, to be obliged to report that the school prospect for some time to come is discouraging. Many of the teachers in the country parishes will not, owing to the above cause, receive any remuneration for their faithful services, but are now, in some instances, destitute of the necessaries of life.

Public schools opposed.—The colored schools, now under the school board in New Orleans, are generally well attended, but their number is entirely too small to accommodate one-half of the colored children in this city. The city council are working against the board to destroy these schools by withholding means for the payment of rents, salaries, supply of books, &c., and even propose to reduce the appropriation given before the addition of the colored schools, one-third; while it should, in justice, be increased at least one-half. Many of the newly appointed teachers have their sympathies engaged only by their salaries, with little care for the permanent improvement of the colored race.

In almost every parish the freedmen are anxious to educate themselves and children, and evince all the earnestness that could be expected, willingly co-operating with those who labor for their advancement; but in many localities the planters will not allow freedmen's schools to be established, and with their opposition it is impossible and unsafe to attempt to open them.

Repairs.—Several school buildings have been repaired at a small expense to the bureau, and every effort is being made to bring the schools of this State back to the prosperous condition in which they were before the overflow and destruction of the crops, and the great interruption of the schools by yellow fever.

There has been little or no charitable aid received by the schools of this State for the past two years. They have struggled on and gradually increased until within the past few months, wholly supported by the freedmen and this bureau.

Pay for teachers.—I am in daily receipt of petitions to open schools for the freedmen in the country districts, and if it were possible for this bureau or northern associations to pay teachers a salary of $40 per month regularly, at least one thousand good free schools, with full attendance, could be opened at once.

J. M. Langston, general inspector, says in a late report:

Moral influence wanting.—It is to be regretted that, according to the method of conducting the schools of New Orleans and throughout the State of Louisiana, almost no moral or religious influences are brought to bear upon the children. In many schools the opening exercise is the ringing of the bell, and the order "get your books and go to studying." In others there is no opening prayer, and no singing of sacred song, the poetry of which impresses a valuable moral lesson. In some of the schools of this city it is different, but in few of them did I find any special effort to cultivate sound morals among the children.

Industry.—Wherever I travelled in Louisiana and met the freedmen I found them industrious, for the most part temperate, and interested in their elevation. I found none of them in such needy circumstances as to require governmental aid, except those who are aged and infirm—the wrecks of slavery—and orphan children. And this was equally true of the freedmen of Alabama generally as I saw them. I found no vagrancy among them. All are anxious to work; they are very generally employed, and many are doing well in the accumulation of property.

TEXAS.

The schools in Texas went on prosperously until about the end of June, and many of the teachers would have remained through the summer, but the fatal epidemic which prevailed brought the schools to a close in all the larger places of the State, and prevented the northern associations from executing the liberal schemes they had formed for the current year.

Sickness and death.—The superintendent of education says:

Early in June the malarial and bilious fevers of the climate had attacked so many of our teachers, particularly those from the north, and the outlook for the summer was so ominous, that it was thought advisable to close the schools with the month. About one-fourth of the teachers, however, decided to remain and continue their work during vacation, but the rapid spread of the epidemic throughout the seaboard and larger towns paralyzed all further efforts. Hundreds of our pupils perished, and at least three faithful teachers. On the return of the healthy season the teachers returned, and the schools, aided by the experience of the past two years, again resumed in a measure their beneficent course.

The decease of the assistant commissioner, the late and lamented Brevet Major General Charles Griffin, who fell a victim to the disease, was one of the afflictive events of the summer. General Griffin was not only an efficient officer, but his whole heart was set upon the elevation of the freedmen. His plans—well matured and comprehensive—were rapidly going into practice. We shall ever regret that the period of his service was so brief, while one of the highest tributes to his memory is the record of what he actually accomplished in the educational interests of Texas.

General Reynolds.—The appointment of his able successor, Brevet Major General J. J. Reynolds, gives promise that the work so well commenced will be resumed and vigorously prosecuted. But the schools must unavoidably for a while suffer, and, under the above circumstances, a gradual approach only to the former attendance can at present be expected.

The highest number of schools of all kinds and pupils during the period covered by this report is, schools, 72; pupils, 2,731.

These consist of 34 regularly reported day or night schools, with 32 teachers and 1,133 pupils, and 5 Sabbath schools, with 394 pupils.

Schools "not regularly reported," but "within the knowledge of the superintendent," are 26 day or night schools, with 30 teachers and 689 pupils, and 7 Sabbath schools, with 13 teachers and 515 pupils.

Eleven of the buildings used for school purposes are owned entirely by the freed people, and 24 of the schools are sustained wholly or in part by them.

The above schools are in charge of 75 teachers, of whom 39 are white and 36 colored.

Of the whole number of pupils, 105 are in the alphabet, 265 spell and read easy lessons, 420 are advanced readers, 155 are in geography, 401 in arithmetic, 511 in writing, and 34 are in the higher branches.

This bureau has expended $1,628 32 for rents, repairs, and material for school buildings, and the amount expended by all parties for the support of the above schools has been $2,092 32.

We are confident that Texas will have a return of liberal patronage from abroad, the disasters of the last year producing deeper sympathy; and that the educational interests of the State will soon regain their former character, thus showing, in another striking instance, that freedmen's schools, as an institution, have a vitality which nothing can destroy.

ARKANSAS.

The educational work in this comparatively new State is making rapid progress. The vacation period even was not able to stop it. Sixteen day schools with 683 pupils, and 13 Sabbath schools, with 1,000 pupils, continued through the summer. Much praise is due the superintendent, William M. Colby, esquire, for his efficient administration of affairs.

There are now in Arkansas schools of all kinds, 52; pupils, 3,361.

Eighteen of these are regularly reported day or night schools, with 31 teachers and 1,006 pupils; 16 are Sabbath schools, with 44 teachers and 1,625 pupils, and 1 industrial school, with 35 pupils.

Seven are irregularly reported day or night schools, with 10 teachers and 295 pupils; and 10 are Sabbath schools, reported in the same way, with 22 teachers and 400 pupils.

Eighteen schools are sustained wholly or in part by the freedmen, and they own 10 of the buildings in which schools are held. Tuition in the aggregate of $1,470 80 has been paid by 346 of the pupils, averaging a fraction over $4 25 per scholar.

For rents and repairs of school buildings this bureau has paid $516 17, and for the support of the above schools by all parties $4,481 25 has been expended.

Of the above pupils 724 spell and read easy lessons, 233 are in advanced readers, 156 are in geography, 375 in arithmetic, 400 in writing, and 60 are in the higher branches.

The whole number of teachers employed is 107, 60 white and 47 colored.

The reports of General C. H. Smith, assistant commissioner, show how inviting the field is for an increased number of schools, and appeal strongly to the educational associations for more teachers.

Plantation schools.—Many more schools (he says) could be established if we had teachers of the right sort. A person with a common education and humble pretensions could go on the plantations where there are from 50 to 125 freedmen of all classes, and sustain a school all the year round at a very comfortable compensation.

The agent for Chicot county, in which there are no schools, says he would establish four plantation schools at once if he had the teachers. The agent for Sevier county also gives the names of four plantations on which the proprietors are desirous of having schools, and offer to furnish school-rooms and board for teachers in their families free of charge as an inducement.

Increase.—The common and Sabbath schools continue in a prosperous condition, both increasing in number and interest. The great drawbacks are the want of good teachers and money to pay them with. The freedmen themselves are poor, yet very anxious to learn, and are making great sacrifices to obtain an education. The school-houses in course of erection are rapidly approaching completion; all of them will be ready for use early in the autumn.

In September the superintendent reports 16 schools in operation, attended by 683 pupils, and 13 Sabbath schools, with an enrolment of 1,000.

Graded school.—The school-house at Little Rock has been completed and supplied with desks of the most improved pattern and at less cost to the government than a much inferior article could be furnished. Early in October the building will be dedicated and occupied by a full force of teachers from the Indiana Yearly Meeting of Friends. It will be the first graded school for colored people in Arkansas.

The freedmen have elected a board of education from among their own number to take charge of the building and the school. This board has already assumed one-half the current expenses, thereby relieving the Friends of a portion of the heavy burden which they have for two years so generously borne for the benefit of this people.

The building at Helena has been supplied with furniture similar to that at Little Rock, and will also be occupied by the Friends in October.

School buildings are much needed at Fayetteville, Fort Smith, Camden, Van Buren, and a score of smaller places.

Encouragement.—In October the superintendent says :

There is cause for encouragement, although our work has not extended rapidly. Our means of communication are so uncertain owing to the nature of the country, the absence of railroads and the prevalence of high water during long periods, that it requires a long time to accomplish small results. Another obstacle to the progress of our work is the lack of energy that prevails among all classes. The freedmen are anxious for schools. The planters often admit that the enlightenment of the laborers is just the best thing for themselves and their country; but when the importance of action is urged, imbecility or constitutional inertia prevents them from making the necessary steps to have schools planted in their vicinity.

Expense for the year.—Expense of schools the last year has been $9,798 19, of which nothern societies have contributed $6,470, and the freedmen themselves $3,370.

Great improvement is seen in school accommodations by the generous appropriation of Congress through the bureau.

Buildings have been erected, or are now in process of erection, at the following points :

Little Rock, at a cost of	$5,300 00
Pine Bluff, at a cost of	3,575 00
Helena, at a cost of	3,711 00
Washington, at a cost of	2,500 00
Batesville, at a cost of	2,480 00

White schools stimulated.—Already the work of educating the freedmen is stimulating white citizens to do something for the education of their own children. The city of Little Rock having no public schools hitherto, has just voted an appropriation for the first public school-house within her limits.

In November, a large gain was made. The report shows an increased enrolment of fifty per cent. in day schools, and seventy-five per cent. in Sabbath schools, over the preceding month.

Receipts for tuition were over 100 dollars in excess of the October receipts.

In the "Union school" at Little Rock, alone, there has been a net increase of 100 pupils.

Cotton crop.—Two successive failures of the cotton crop, coupled with the extremely low price of that staple, have ruined hundreds of planters, and left thousands of freedmen as destitute as they were two years ago. Many planters who would be just to the freedmen, are scarcely able to supply their own families with bread, much less to feed their laborers ; while the avaricious and unscrupulous, disappointed in their expected gains, leave no stone unturned to swindle the poor freedman out of his share of the meagre crops. In this state or affairs it is not surprising that with the freedmen the question of *food for their children* takes precedence of that of their education.

A school-house has been opened in a homestead settlement 10 miles from this city. The freedmen erected a small building for the purpose, and furnished a home for a teacher. They have been quite energetic, and desire a permanent school.

Public sentiment.—With great satisfaction I report increasing friendliness towards our work and teachers. This is especially noticeable in the larger towns. As one evidence of this, the city authorities of Little Rock have recently voted to pay over the amount of school tax collected from the colored citizens to the bureau Superintendent of Education, to be used for the exclusive benefit of the colored schools.

This last step, though but an act of justice, is certainly quite in advance of former times in Arkansas.

TENNESSEE.

In Tennessee comparatively good school laws have been enacted, but are not executed with such practical effect as to give the freedmen their intended benefits.

Much local prejudice against the elevation of the colored race still exists. There needs to be a radical change in the general sentiments of society, a change also in industrial pursuits and institutions, in order that education for all may take its legitimate place in popular estimation and patronage.

The schools for freedmen, however, commenced promptly after the summer vacation, and are going on with comparative prosperity.

The reports show that the numbers of all kinds, and of pupils, have already reached the following:

Schools... 221
Pupils.. 13, 145

Of these, 127 are day or night schools, with 140 teachers and 6,172 pupils; 66 Sabbath schools, with 356 teachers and 6,178 pupils; and eight industrial schools, with 195 pupils. There are six high or normal schools, so called, with 180 pupils. These are included among the above day schools.

To these are added the irregularly reported schools, consisting of 20 day or night schools, with 20 teachers and 600 pupils.

Forty-five of the above schools are in grades from one to four.

The average attendance of pupils in the day or night schools has been 4,568, or 74 per cent.

Of the whole number of teachers engaged, 276 are white and 240 colored; 147 of these have been furnished transportation by this bureau.

The freedmen themselves own 37 of the school buildings, and sustain, wholly or in part, 81 of the schools.

There has been paid by 2,903 of the pupils in the day or night schools $5,663 83, making an average tuition fee of about $1 95 per scholar.

This bureau has expended in Tennessee for rental and repairs, including material for school buildings, $10,283 19; and all parties have contributed for the support of the above schools, $25,034 86.

School law.—The assistant commissioner, General W. P. Carlin, reports that a school law has been adopted which promises equal advantages to all children in disbursing the school fund. But this law has not yet gone into practical effect.

The State still prohibits colored men from holding office and sitting on juries. These are the only discriminations against them now on the statute-books of Tennessee.

Nearly all the schools in operation before vacation are again opened, with prospects of several more during the coming months.

In some of the counties the young children will be kept busy for some time picking cotton.

Bitter feeling.—The state of feeling among the people who were rebels is very bitter, more so than a year ago. They actually hate every one who differs from them in opinion, and would do them any injury in their power.

Private schools.—It is a noticeable fact that the freedmen are opening many private schools which they propose to sustain, but over which they ask the bureau superintendent of education to exercise supervision.

A recent enrolment of colored children of school age, in Nashville, gives 2,216, and only 450 of these are in the schools established by the city. The remainder are left for charity and private schools.

It is openly said in many communities that there is no room for teachers from the north. In West Tennessee a teacher lately disappeared under circumstances exciting the suspicion that he was murdered. He had previously been assaulted in the street.

Politicians.—In many instances men who have been elevated to office by the support of the negroes, care nothing for their education, and offer no suggestions or encouragement to schools, until the bureau undertakes the work. Then they are ready to step in when it will cost them nothing, and, if possible, gain the credit of the movement in the estimation of the colored people.

In many communities, however, the schools are in the hands of good men, who are frequently called to the exercise of great moral courage in carrying through the enterprise. The prompt co-operation of the bureau is necessary in most instances.

The field for our efforts in this region is becoming more and more open every month, through the awakening desires of the colored people for schools, and a growing conviction on the part of the whites that they must be allowed to have them.

New system of labor wanted.—The expectation that Tennessee will soon rally, and secure instructions necessary to a high degree of prosperity for our schools, is not to be speedily realized. There must be a new system of agriculture; the establishment of manufactures and a regeneration in the common methods of labor. The impoverished state, in which popular ignorance is so prevalent, will not practice retrenchment upon the plans which the few who feel the importance of education may propose. Consider, with this fact, the special prejudice which exists in respect to the negroes, and nothing is more certain than that they will remain in ignorance unless the general government shall continue and enlarge its present efforts for their intellectual improvement.

Well planned agencies for education in its widest sense must be furnished. The freedmen must be led out of the wilderness of ignorance, if it takes 40 years. We are under peculiar obligations to these people, which, if not discharged, retribution will come to us through their poverty and crime, and, perhaps, in the end, the popular violence which must be the result.

Fisk School. —At Nashville the Fisk School has grown into the Fisk University, incorporated by the State. The grounds are eligibly located. The buildings, formerly used as a military hospital, are quite extensive, and, when properly furnished, will accommodate 1,200 to 1,500 pupils. The rooms are large, well lighted and ventilated; the court-yards within the walls handsomely sodded, and the whole appearance of the place is neat and attractive. The institution embraces three departments, preparatory, normal, and collegiate, and is supplied with an efficient corps of teachers. The property was purchased in 1866 by the American Missionary Association and the Western Freedmen's Aid Commission, at a cost of $16,000.

Great and permanent good is expected from this rising institution, in furnishing teachers and leading men for the colored population of Tennessee.

KENTUCKY.

In Kentucky, which did not engage in the rebellion as a State, and where the bureau has, therefore, had but little power, peculiar embarrassments have existed. Local prejudice has been intense. The freedmen, who in great numbers enlisted in the Union army, returned brave and manly, but poor, and many of them homeless.

A large amount of benevolent aid was needed, while but little has been received. It was unsafe for the educational associations to spend money where they could not be thoroughly protected. But, through the energy of bureau officers, and especially of the superintendent, Reverend T. K. Noble, the schools have grown, and, at this date, they are nearly equal in numbers and attendance to the best period of last year.

All kinds of schools, as reported, 218 ; pupils 13,980, including 120 regular day or night schools, with 145 teachers and 6,493 pupils ; and 83 Sabbath schools with 6,343 pupils. One high or normal school with 225 pupils is reported with the day schools.

There are, also, in the whole number, but not regularly reported, eight day or night schools, with 18 teachers and 480 pupils ; and seven Sabbath schools with 37 teachers and 664 pupils. Thirty-five of the day schools are graded, viz : primary, intermediate, and grammar.

Of the 200 teachers in charge of the above schools 39 are white and 161 colored.

The average attendance has been 5,220, or 80 per cent.

Tuition, amounting in the aggregate to $6,897, has been paid by 3,973 of the pupils, making an average of over $173 per scholar.

The amount from all sources, for the support of the above schools, has been $13,334 91.

This bureau has expended $5,364 99 for rents and repairs, including material for school buildings.

Forty-one of the school houses are owned entirely by the freedmen, and they support, wholly or in part, 117 of the schools.

The yearly report of General Sidney Burbank, assistant commissioner, in October, has a summary of interesting facts :

Continuous struggle. —The freedmen of Kentucky, in their efforts to give their children the rudiments of an education, have had a continuous struggle with poverty. Thrown by the "proclamation of emancipation" upon their own resources, compelled to assume the responsibilities of freedmen, with no previous preparation or discipline ; without friends ; without property ; hearing on all sides from their old masters the continuous prophecy that their race was certain to die off in a few years; allowed no voice in the assessment of their taxes; cheated, assaulted, mobbed; it has been a marvel that they have had heart to do anything for the education of their children. Only by great prudence, incessant labor, and a careful saving of every dime, have they been able to supply themselves with the bare necessaries of life. But poverty and ill treatment have not been the only obstacles which have confronted them.

Opposition.—There has been special and most bitter opposition on the part of white citizens to the education of colored children; and this hostility has done much to dishearten the freedmen, and thwart the efforts of the officers of this bureau in organizing and sustaining schools. These men have persistently and publicly ridiculed the very idea of educating the negro; they have threatened to destroy any buildings that might be had for school purposes, and, I have no doubt, would have carried out their threat but for the presence of United States troops.

There has been still another hinderance to the extension of the educational work, viz : the small amount of aid rendered by the benevolent associations of the country. The managers of these organizations have doubtless felt that it was the part of wisdom to make their appropriations where they would be better appreciated. The result has been that while the freedmen of Tennessee have received during the year from benevolence an average of more than $6,000 a month, the freedmen of Kentucky have received from the same source only about $600 a month.

Growth.—But in spite of the hinderances above mentioned the work has gone on rapidly. There has been great improvement in the management of these schools; incompetent and unfaithful teachers have been removed and their places filled, as far as possible, by teachers trained for the work.

Only a beginning.—Only a beginning, however, has been made. There are in the State more than 37,000 colored children between the ages of 6 and 18 years. Five thousand only of these are in the schools, while 32,000 are growing up in ignorance.

The only practicable course seems to be, to establish first-class schools at all central points, making them, as far as possible, model schools; and then follow close in the wake of public sentiment in the smaller settlements; assist the freedmen to erect school houses wherever there is reason to believe they will not be destroyed; put these schools in operation and help sustain them, until the freedmen are able to sustain them themselves.

Teachers of their own race.—There must also be schools in the State for the training of teachers for these thousands of untaught children. Here in Kentucky the colored people generally prefer that teachers should belong to their own race. They will accept white teachers in virtue of their superior qualifications, but whenever they can get black ones really competent, they receive them with great satisfaction. During the past year I have had to look mainly to Oberlin for colored teachers really fit for the work.

In compliance with instructions contained in circular letter dated Washington, June 26, 1867, I now submit some of the more prominent points which the progress of the work has developed:

1st. A persistent determination on the part of the freedmen to educate their children. Nothing has surprised me more than to see this people, held in bondage all their lives and shut out from all avenues of knowledge, rising at once to the conception of the worth of an education, and resolving at all hazards that their children shall have it. Of course there are many exceptions. Many worthless persons take no interest at all in these schools, but the great majority of parents seem resolved that whatever else they fail to obtain, their children must be instructed.

2d. Capacity of the children for education. This question has been conclusively settled by the experience of the past year. No fair-minded man who is familiar with schools will fail to admit that, all things considered, the progress of these pupils will compare favorably with that of white children.

3d. The secret of this progress and of the interest of the parents in the schools is found in the fact that the *consciousness of freedom* has taken hold of them. When parents come to me and ask for the establishment of schools, their plea is, "You know, sir, we are citizens now, and we want to learn our duty." When I visit the schools and ask the children why they are so anxious to learn, the answer is, "because we are citizens, now, sir." This central thought which seems to run through all they do, that they are no longer chattels, but citizens, is itself a great educator.

4th. Necessity of constant oversight. This people know the worth of knowledge. They are thoroughly in earnest in their efforts to obtain it, but they must be shown the way and shown it continually. They are not used to taking the responsibility of directing affairs. For some time to come, therefore, they will need the help of organizing and directing minds. Otherwise their efforts will be more or less a failure.

Little needs to be added to the above full synopsis of school affairs in Kentucky. The points are clearly stated, and should impress the good people of that State with their importance.

The superintendent says:

The inspections ordered have been promptly and thoroughly made, and a large number of towns indicated where schools ought to be organized. Twenty-three schools have been started in these places.

We regret being obliged to add the evidences of continued hostility which he gives:

A petition has been sent to the city authorities in Louisville, praying that the new school house on Broadway, now nearly completed, be purchased by the city, upon the assertion that the building is a nuisance—although confessedly one of the finest school houses in the city—because it is to be used for the education of the negro. Threats have been repeatedly made that it shall be burned, and a guard is stationed over it day and night.

Opposition everywhere.—I greatly fear that when government officers are removed, many of the schools, now in successful operation in the interior of the State, will be broken up. I see this opposition to the schools everywhere. Where they have been in successful operation for some time the opposition is least, and I think in time it will wholly cease; but that time is not yet.

The superintendent gives many cases of hostility in different parts of the State:

Almost every school in Louisville has been interfered with in one way or another since the first of July, 1867. In seven of the schools instances of interference have been reported. In many portions of the Louisville sub-district, such is the hostility it would be positively unsafe for an officer or an agent of the bureau to openly undertake to organize a school without protection.

Lexington sub-district.—C. J. True, who has charge of six counties in the northern portion of the district, reports much opposition to colored schools in many of the towns, and specifies a number of places where schools ought to be organized, but where the hostility is so intense they could be carried on only under the immediate protection of United States troops.

Welsh clergyman.—As an illustration of the intense hostility in the southern sub-district: The freedmen, with the assistance of $150 from this bureau, put up a neat school-house, and a Welsh clergyman was sent there as teacher. When this was known he was driven from the hotel and compelled to take up his quarters with a colored man. Soon after, the house of this colored man was surrounded by a mob, who demanded the teacher and threatened to batter down the doors if they were not immediately admitted. Before they could carry out their threat a squad of soldiers made their appearance, and the mob dispersed. The commanding officer of the troops then gave the teacher a tent within the limits of the camp, and when necessary a guard of soldiers.

Hostility malignant.—The malignant hostility of white citizens, not of the better, the more intelligent class, possibly not of the majority, is the one great impediment to the general education of the freedmen all over the State. It shows itself in constant efforts to prejudice the negroes towards those who are seeking to help them. They are told that "all the teachers want is their money." That "schools will do them no good." That it is "much better to have their children earn money than to waste their time at school."

I beg leave respectfully to say that if the officers and agents of the bureau are dispensed with at present, a persecution of the freedmen will be inaugurated which will be in many respects worse than his former state of slavery.

In many towns in the interior of the State it has been found impossible to either hire buildings for colored schools, or to secure a lot of land whereon to build them. School-houses have been destroyed and the lives of teachers threatened. It is absolutely impossible to secure board for white teachers; still there has been progress, and our teachers deserve great credit for their perseverance.

Colored teachers.—The almost exclusive employment of colored teachers in this State at first involved the necessity of putting into the work those who were very imperfectly prepared. But, as a majority of the children were in the alphabet, these teachers, poorly qualified as they were, rendered good service.

Normal school at Berea.—At Berea, Madison county, four new buildings, by the aid of the bureau, have been erected and are now completed. Two of them are of large capacity. The attendance at the school is 240. Nearly one-half of the pupils are white. A normal department has been established, and a large number of young men and women are receiving special training with a view to their becoming teachers.

Cairo.—Extracts from a special report on schools in Cairo, Illinois, are appended:

In the city of Cairo there are 400 or 500 children of freedmen between the ages of 6 and 18 years. Hitherto no provision whatever has been made for their education.

A large proportion of these are refugees from Kentucky, who went to Cairo soon after the breaking out of the war, and, as a class, are poor.

These people have recently raised $1,500 by subscription towards the construction of a school building; and three contiguous lots have been donated by the trustees of city property, on condition that a brick building be erected thereon, which shall cost not less than $8,000.

The freedmen are determined that the enterprise shall succeed, and their trustees believe they can raise among themselves $1,000, one-half of the amount required. If General Howard can aid them to an equal amount the enterprise will be a success.

Continuance of the bureau.—During the past six months I have visited all parts of the State. I know the situation of the freedmen, and the sentiments of the white citizens, and I respectfully submit that the removal of the bureau in this State will, in my judgment, not only put a stop to all further extension of the educational work, but will result in the breaking up of many schools now in successful operation. I ask attention to this significant fact. For the first time since my connection with the work my monthly report shows a *decrease* in the aggregate attendance. Up to the present time each month has shown a gain over the previous months; but the news has spread all over the State that the bureau is to be removed, and the freedmen are intimidated.

Six schools have been discontinued and the aggregate attendance of all is diminished. Men who hate the negro are emboldened. Only to-day the news comes that another school-house has been burned at Haysville. Some of the best teachers in the State have assured me that they shall not attempt to continue their schools without the protection of the officers of the bureau.

The secretaries of the American Missionary Association and Western Freedmen's Aid Commission notified me last week that in case the bureau was removed they should no longer be able to send me teachers. They also stated that those already engaged, and for whom transportation had been furnished, were now unwilling to take the risk.

In view of these facts I respectfully and earnestly urge, for the sake of 37,000 colored children of Kentucky, that the bureau be not yet discontinued.

MISSOURI AND KANSAS.

Statistical reports from this district give the number of all kinds of schools 104. pupils 6,885.

Thirty-three of these are day or night schools, taught by 53 teachers and having an attendance of 2,537 pupils; 26 Sabbath schools, with 78 teachers and 1,798 pupils; and 45 irregularly reported day and night schools, with 2,550 pupils.

The average attendance in the day and night schools has been 1,800, or about 70 per cent.

Of the whole number of teachers reported 69 are white and 62 colored.

The freedmen sustain, wholly or in part, 19 of the above schools.

Of the pupils 545 are in the alphabet, 930 spell and read easy lessons, 1,190 are in advanced readers, 574 study geography, 1,057 arithmetic, 1,254 are in writing, and 245 in the higher branches.

A small tuition fee has been paid by 413 of the pupils.

For rents, repairs, and material for school buildings this bureau has expended during the six months $7,700 86.

The superintendent of education, Brevet Lieutenant Colonel F. A. Seely, who is also disbursing officer, states that—

The number of schools reported is small compared with the number ascertained to be actually in operation. I hope to be able to present, before the winter is over, complete statistics for the entire States of Missouri and Kansas.

The amount of disbursements during the month has been entirely for rents and repairs of school buildings, and is as follows:

Missouri..$130 00
Kansas...471 34

Total...601 34

An appropriation of $200 in aid of a school in this city (St. Louis) has not all been expended, but will be in a few days. This may result in securing the permanent establishment of this school under the auspices of the public school board.

With a similar view, I have in one or two instances assisted societies in establishing schools at points where they appeared to be especially needed, and with a reasonable prospect of their being maintained after aid from the bureau shall have ceased. A public school once established is rarely discontinued.

At Warrensburg, Kansas City, and Westport, in buildings erected either wholly or in part by the aid of the bureau, schools will in future be maintained by public school boards without foreign aid.

Progress in 70 counties.—There has been greater progress in educating the freedmen than I imagined at date of my semi-annual report. I have received communications from the superintendents of public schools in 70 counties out of 113 in the State, giving information of great interest.

During a portion of the past year 36 schools for freedmen—public and private—have been carried on, besides those from which I had received reports. In many counties the freedmen are too scattered to admit the establishment of separate schools; but in every county where their number and contiguity warrant it, one or more schools have been opened.

All that the laws will give.—County superintendents manifest great interest in the cause, and are determined to secure to the freedmen all that the laws of the State will give them. These laws provide for an appointment of the school fund *pro rata* with the number of children, white and black. In some instances in the most populous counties no enumeration has been made; and in others, notwithstanding the enumeration, the law has been disregarded, and the portion of funds belonging to the colored people has been appropriated by township boards for white scholars. In some counties where the amount is considerable I have urged the colored people to demand what belongs to them, and in case of refusal to seek redress through the courts. There can be no doubt about the result, and I am desirous to have the matter tested effectually.

A simple decision of the supreme court compelling school boards to refund amounts fairly belonging to freedmen which have been misappropriated, or, if possible, giving reasonable damages for deprivation of school privileges, would result in all our towns and cities in a vast pecuniary benefit to the freedmen.

Bounty money for schools.—Captain Albert L. Aubin has assisted me in the payments of bounties to soldiers throughout the State. He inspires confidence from having been an officer of colored troops and also by coming among the freedmen as a paymaster. He is everywhere counselling them to spend a portion of the money they receive for their own education and that of their children, and especially urging the establishment of night schools. Although not directly employed in school business, I look upon him as a most efficient aid in this branch of my duties.

Liberal spirit.—In Missouri and Kansas freedmen's schools will soon be not only provided for by law, but taken charge of efficiently by public boards.

These two States are both imbued with a liberal spirit towards their colored population. A majority of their white citizens are ready to lay the foundations of universal education, and public sentiment in these younger States has peculiar vitality. With a people, many of them from the best classes of the north and east, these States have received all the elements of free institutions, and citizens native to the soil, or from the south, indicate a readiness to exchange their prejudices for ideas of enlightened progress. This is in pleasant contrast with the somewhat different temper in which our work has been welcomed by the eastern border States. We hope the latter may soon imitate the better model of the west.

GENERAL SURVEY.

With all that is thrilling in the history of the freedmen's education, and encouraging in their progress throughout every district during the period now reported, we are still compelled to say that embarrassments from the revived rebel spirit of the South, as seen in the facts stated, have of late thickened about our schools. The partial withdrawment of the bureau from the border States, and its threatened discontinuance wholly, have had disheartening effect upon superintendents and teachers. The following from a recent communication expresses undoubtedly the truth:

Never was the spirit of opposition more bitter and defiant than at the present time. The civil authorities, being in sympathy with this feeling, wink at all outrages; and the military, located at a few points, are often entirely unable to reach the perpetrators of wrongs. Under these circumstances you will not be surprised to learn that many of our teachers are discouraged and are unwilling to return to their fields for the coming year. The truth is, we are in the midst of a reign of terror, and unless something is done and done speedily for the relief of the persecuted Union people and friends of humanity, our educational work and interests must seriously suffer.

Had not these schools the inherent elements of life, vigorous life, which grow in spite of adverse influences, they would be quite paralyzed. As it is, they continue in a prosperous condition, and in spite of opposition their course is still onward.

The State constitutions now being framed by the southern conventions will all contain liberal provisions for universal education, and it is a " consummation devoutly to be wished" that these may become the established law of all these States.

Adult education.—Adult freed people, especially the men, are earnestly seeking that instruction which will fit them for their new responsibilities. Evening schools for adults, of great utility, are becoming more and more numerous; often conducted by volunteer friends of the colored race, and with a modesty which forbids making public mention of their work. Over five hundred of these evening schools are now in operation.

Moral condition.—The moral condition of freedmen has not been overlooked. All teachers are required to carefully watch the habits of their children, rebuking vice and encouraging virtue. This result is reached more especially in Sabbath schools. These, as seen from the returns, have been operated throughout the entire south, reaching tens of thousands who cannot attend upon weekday teaching. We have now nearly 1,500 of these schools. They are often described in the regular reports.

Remaining want.—Only about one-seventh of the children of freedmen are as yet receiving any kind of instruction, and we call especial attention to the following statement : By the census of 1860 there were in the field covered by the operations of this bureau 1,664,600 colored persons of *suitable school* age, *i. e.*, between 5 and 20 years ; and a census taken now would not differ much from the above.

The whole present number of pupils in our schools, as reported during the best portion of last year, including older persons, with 1,348 white pupils, and large numbers duplicated in the several kinds of schools, was but 238,342.

Now, if, in view of all who may be studying outside of the schools, we can double this number, then less than half a million of freed persons have commenced to learn from books. Deduct these from the children and youth who are of suitable school age as given above, and there are left 1,187,916 of this class wholly unprovided for, enough to make 23,738 schools of 50 pupils each.

Census of want.—The following table shows how these destitute youth and children are distributed through the several States, as estimated upon the census of 1860 and our present statistics of freedmen's schools. It is believed to be substantially correct :

States.	Colored population of school age.	Number in school.	Number not in school.	Ratio in school.
Delaware	8,726	1,789	6,937	1 to 5
Maryland, District Columbia, and West Virginia	78,944	30,030	48,914	3 to 7
Virginia	210,279	27,659	182,620	1 to 8
North Carolina	150,769	24,291	126,478	1 to 6
South Carolina	162,806	29,083	133,723	1 to 6
Georgia	187,502	25,779	161,723	1 to 7
Florida	24,529	4,204	20,325	1 to 6
Alabama	173,204	18,159	155,045	1 to 9
Mississippi	163,762	10,402	153,360	1 to 15
Louisiana	115,861	17,469	98,392	1 to 7
Texas	74,701	7,364	67,337	1 to 10
Arkansas	44,418	4,710	39,708	1 to 9
Tennessee	118,410	16,508	101,902	1 to 7
Kentucky	99,553	13,704	85,849	1 to 7
Missouri and Kansas	51,136	7,191	43,945	1 to 7
Total	1,664,600	238,342	1,426,258	1 to 7

CONFERENCE OF FREEDMEN'S SOCIETIES IN NEW YORK.

A conference was held on the 10th day of September, 1867, at No. 30 Vesey street, New York city, at which the following societies were represented :

The American Freedmen's Union Commission, the Baltimore branch, the Pennsylvania branch, the New England branch, the New York branch, the American Missionary Association, and the Friends' Freedmen's Association of Philadelphia.

The object of the meeting was to devise a plan for securing the co-operation of the freed people with the northern societies in the support of the schools.

After a report on the subject, and free discussion of the topics named, the following resolutions were passed :

1. *Resolved*, That the best interests of the freed people require the permanent establishment of free schools in the south; that, as in the northern free-school system, the people should co-operate in their support; and, therefore, that no new school should be established except where co-operation can be secured.

2. *Resolved*, That our teachers and agents in the South should organize the people into associations to raise means to aid in the establishment and support of their schools.

3. *Resolved*, That, in the opinion of this meeting, all books should be sold at a price to be fixed by the teachers' committee.

This bureau will co-operate heartily in carrying out the above resolutions, and we have, in a circular letter, called the attention of our State superintendents to them.

SCHOOL DISTRICTS.

The last topic suggests that the time has come when the efforts of the freedmen to educate themselves should take some organized and efficient form. There is now a willingness on their part to bear a large share of the expense, but how to put schools in operation is the practical difficulty. They should be taught to do this for themselves. When the south organizes public school systems, to be sustained by the permanent funds of the State, or by taxation, whatever the freedmen may have done in this direction will aid rather than hinder such State effort. The educational associations and this bureau are still ready to help especially such as help themselves; but some popular plan is needed by which this aid shall be co-operative with the efforts of the freedmen, and which shall gradually teach them to be self-reliant.

We propose, therefore, to have school districts formed from four to six miles square, overspreading all the interior parts of the State. Large towns and cities can modify this plan. All adult males would be voters in these districts, and with such aid as could be procured would proceed at once to build a school-house, becoming, as a body, permanently responsible for carrying on a school therein.

Teachers, of course, must be provided; but these will be forthcoming when called for, and we have reasons to believe that the normal schools now commencing throughout the south will, before long, furnish these in numbers equal to the demand.

Aid in many other respects may be needed at first to carry out this plan. Public meetings of the freedmen will be necessary. The bureau superintendents and sub-assistant commissioners will have to originate and attend many of the primary gatherings; and to perfect the work perhaps a special field agent may be called for, to aid in the organization of the districts and bringing them into working shape.

We are sure such a plan, with proper effort, will succeed. The schools will then assume a fixed shape and permanent character; their increase being a native growth, and even in their primitive shape acquiring vigor by calling out the resources of the people themselves. These districts would be models for the whole population, ready at hand to unite with any equitable State system whenever instituted.

The death of large numbers of the adult colored population in the late war has left to our care a greater number of parentless colored children in the south than is the usual proportion in any population under ordinary circumstances. Much has been done by the bureau for these orphans.

In the asylum at Charleston, South Carolina, there are at present 115 children, varying in age from a few weeks or months to nine or ten years. This establishment is well kept, and always found in good condition.

There are two orphan asylums in Arkansas, one at Little Rock, in connection with the hospital, and one 10 miles west of Helena, also in connection with that hospital. They were both recently transferred to the charge of the bureau from the "Indiana Yearly Meeting of Friends." The Little Rock asylum contained, August 31, 1867, 29 inmates, of which number 15 were colored males, 7 colored females, and 3 white males, and 4 white females.

An asylum, located about eight miles from Wilmington, North Carolina, was established in May, 1866, and for which the bureau furnishes rations. Since its organization, 137 orphans have been provided for.

The asylum of the Orphan's Home Society, in Louisiana, furnishes the following data: Male children from 3 months to 14 years of age, 54; female children from 3 months to 14 years of age, 30.

The number of orphans in Virginia under charge of the bureau is 119.

North Carolina has the Brewer Asylum. Since it was founded, June, 1866, 150 orphans and destitute children have been cared for therein. Fifty-five are now there, 42 of whom are under 14 years of age.

An asylum for the aged and infirm and permanently disabled, and orphan children, has been for a long time established at Freedman's Village, Arlington, Virginia, where many of the above had been collected by the quartermasters' department during the war. The bureau has the entire charge of this institution. Number of inmates in September, 1867:

Men	178
Women	245
Male children	84
Female children	90
Total	597

Those who are able have assisted in working a vegetable garden, and some of the women have been employed at the industrial school.

The Colored Orphan's House, of Washington, District of Columbia, under the auspices of the Ladies' National Association, for the relief of destitute colored women and children, has been in successful operation in a new building, constructed for it by this bureau.

Number of aged women at the Home January, 1868	5
Number of orphans, (same date)	84
Total	89

An excellent matron is in charge, with her assistants and teachers. The routine is that of a well-disciplined family, and the school in which the children are daily assembled is among the best of its grade in the city. Places are found for these orphans in good families in the north and west as soon as it can be judiciously done, and thus a stream is constantly coming from abodes of wretchedness and going to conditions of comfort and respectability. The whole number which this asylum received during the last year was 185.

UNFORTUNATE CLASSES.

Consolidated report of medical officers upon the unfortunate classes in all the States under this bureau.

These nearly 3,000 afflicted persons appeal to our sympathy and should be provided for. There is a peculiar education which they can receive and which will greatly alleviate their condition. The several States, when reconstructed, will undoubtedly make such provision; some are doing it now. We quote with pleasure the following testimony of General Scott, of South Carolina:

There is no legal restriction to the admission of colored people to the insane asylum of this State. I found several receiving treatment in a building adjoining the Charleston hospital. Considering the accommodations insufficient for their proper care, I requested the mayor of the city to have them transferred to the asylum at Columbia. With that request he promptly complied, and since then all similar cases have been immediately transferred to that institution at the expense of the civil authorities. The local authorities throughout the State are required to provide for their insane in the same manner.

TEMPERANCE ORGANIZATIONS.

There are now connected with our schools 44 children's temperance societies, called the "Vanguard of Freedom," having, in the aggregate, 3,000 members. These societies are constantly increasing, and are doing much to train their members in all correct moral habits; the pledge forbidding not only "intoxicating spirits," but "tobacco and all profane and vulgar language."

We have reason to believe that temperance among all classes of the freedmen will prevail. The assistant commissioner of South Carolina says:

Temperance is a predominant feature among the freed people of this district. A freedman or woman under the influence of liquor is a rarity.

The assistant commissioner of Florida testifies that—

The institution of temperance societies under instructions contained in circular letter from the commissioner of the bureau, May 15, 1867, has been attended with a great degree of success. Officers have worked mainly through religious bodies and schools in their organization. At present there are few towns of any importance in the State without an established society.

The superintendent of education for Arkansas reports:

As auxiliary to the educational work, the existence of several temperance organizations in the State, aggregating a membership of about 500.

There were three societies organized in St. Francis county the present month, (September,) and another society at Helena numbering 150 members. This society was the first among the freedmen in the State and is the result of the labors of a missionary teacher.

I hail these efforts to suppress inebriety as auguries of the coming of the better time when the appetites and passions of the freed people shall be subordinate to the moral faculties and the intellect.

Mr. Langston says:

In North Carolina the habit of whiskey drinking and the use of tobacco among the freedmen are too prevalent; yet I may safely report improvement in this particular. I apprehend that reform as to the use of both whiskey and tobacco will move on rapidly as soon as the temperance societies known as "Vanguards of Freedom" are organized in the schools. Superintendent Fiske assured me that this work should be taken up at once.

SAVINGS BANKS.

Education in thrift and economy is effected through the influence of the Freedmen's Savings and Trust Company, chartered by Congress, and placed under the protection of this bureau. Twenty branches of this institution, located in as many of the central cities and large towns of the southern States, are now in operation. Six of these banks have at this time, January 1, 1868, on deposit an average of over $50,000 each, the whole amount due depositors at all the branches being $585,770 17. Four times this amount has been deposited for a time, and then drawn out for use in important purchases, homesteads, &c. Both the business and influence of the bank are rapidly increasing.

Multitudes of these people never before had the first idea of saving for future use. Their former industry was only a hard, profitless task; but under the influence of these savings banks the value of money is learned, and they are stimulated to earn it. Their savings already give assurance that as a people the freedmen are destined to rise superior to want ; the majority to possess every substantial comfort, and many to attain affluence.

We receive much valuable testimony as to the benign influence of this institution.

General Miles, of North Carolina, says :

The establishment of savings banks, under the charter of the Freedmen's Savings and Trust Company, is one of the designs of the bureau in this State. The matter has been brought to the notice of my officers and will have attention. Other efforts are being made to induce habits of economy among the colored people with considerable success ; and a desire to accumulate property, and thus more firmly establish themselves upon an independent footing, is prevalent.

General Reynolds, of Texas, states that up to the time of the muster-out of colored regiments the representative of the bank attended at all payments made to them ; explained the objects of the institution, and received such moneys as they chose to deposit. The exertions of the agent with these troops undoubtedly saved for them many thousands of dollars, which would otherwise have been squandered.

The amount received in all from troops in Texas was over $200,000 ; this large sum being all transmitted safely to the principal office at Washington, where it still remains, or has been drawn out as these soldiers returning to their homes needed it.

General Sprague says :

The influence of this institution upon the freed people is beneficial in the highest degree.

CONCLUSION.

In conclusion we have to say that the whole record of facts now given shows that deep foundations have been laid for the improvement, not only of the present, but all generations of these freedmen. Earnestly would we appeal to the government, and to the benevolent public, for continued help ; and still more earnestly, if possible, urge these freed people to help themselves. They must struggle long and hard, as in an effort for life. Whether with rights to enjoy or duties to perform, each new opportunity should stimulate to nobler endeavors. The country demands that as citizens these freedmen become intelligent, and He who has delivered them from bondage requires that they practice every virtue. Their sorrows in the past filled all benevolent hearts with sympathy. Will they now in freedom realize the expectations of these friends, and falsify the dark prophecies of their enemies ?

All of which is respectfully submitted.

J. W. ALVORD,
General Superintendent of Schools.

Maj. Gen. O. O. HOWARD, *Commissioner.*

[Circular Letter—No. 3.]

WAR DEPARTMENT,
BUREAU REFUGEES, FREEDMEN AND ABANDONED LANDS,
OFFICE GENERAL SUPERINTENDENT SCHOOLS,
Washington, December 23, 1867.

DEAR SIR : Your attention is called to the following suggestions :

1. Do all you can to make your schools self-supporting by an appeal to local responsibility, and by calling out the means and efforts of the freedmen.

2. Encourage legislation, (State and municipal,) for a *public school system* which shall give educational privileges to all.

Where the State will not act at present, you will assist local voluntary associations whose object is to educate the people irrespective of color.

3. Whenever it is practicable organize the freedmen into school districts, having suitable limits, with a school committee who will be pledged to carry on schools within their respective districts. Such organizations can be aided by this bureau, and by the educational societies of the north.

4. It is desirable that all internal school regulations be perfected—classification, government, methods of teaching, selection of books, and full supply thereof, with special attention to all the habits of pupils, both in and out of school. Please report the *moral condition* of the freedmen in all respects. The teacher's blank, as revised, asks for facts on the subject of temperance.

5. Gather statistics of localities destitute of schools, with the number of children in each between the ages of 6 and 21 years.

6. Report all places where committees or teachers will open schools if a schoolhouse is provided. State the present condition of school buildings. The new blank for sub-assistant commissioners and agents will give much information on these subjects.

7. As far as you can, bring the *adult* population into night and Sabbath schools. Urge all suitable persons, of both colors, to become their teachers. Visit asylums and report what instruction the inmates are receiving.

8. Labor to improve your normal schools. Encourage promising young persons of both sexes to attend and prepare themselves for teaching. Address your advanced schools on this subject.

9. It need not be added that, in all ways, general intelligence among the freedmen is to be encouraged; industry, honesty, and saving habits, as well as a high morality.

10. You will impress upon parents that they are to have a part in this educating work; and the children of the schools should be instructed to exert a good influence *at home* upon brothers, sisters, and parents, conveying to them the knowledge which they themselves are receiving.

I congratulate you in view of success in the past, and unite with you in high hopes for these freed people in whose behalf we are laboring.

Yours, &c., very respectfully.

J. W. ALVORD,
General Superintendent Schools.

[Circular—No. 30.]

WAR DEPARTMENT,
BUREAU REFUGEES, FREEDMEN AND ABANDONED LANDS,
Washington, December 31, 1867.

Hereafter school buildings will not be erected or repaired to any considerable extent at the expense of this bureau, except upon sites secured by deeds to trustees, or some individual party, for school purposes for freedmen, or for children, irrespective of color, forever.

In any exception to this rule, the party owning the building repaired shall give a bond securing the above use, or the building erected shall be placed on temporary piles, (or piers,) and not attached to the soil so as to become a part of the realty.

When buildings for school purposes are built or repaired out of funds or material furnished by this bureau, such funds or material will be accounted for by the proper officers of the bureau.

O. O. HOWARD,
Major General, Commissioner.

[Ed. Form, No. 3.]

Teacher's monthly school report for the month of ———, 186 .

‡ To contain one entire calendar month, and to be forwarded as soon as possible after the close of the month.
‡ A school under the distinct control of one teacher, or a teacher with one assistant, is to be reported as one school.

[*Answers placed here.*]

Name of your school?
Is it a day or night school?
When did your present session commence?
Is your school supported by an educational society?
Is your school supported wholly by local school board?
Is your school supported in part by local school board?
Is your school supported wholly by the freedmen?
Is your school supported in part by the freedmen?
Have you had bureau transportation this term?
Who owns the school building?
Is rent paid by the Freedmen's Bureau?
What number of teachers and assistants in your school?
Total enrolment for the month?
Number enrolled last report?
Number left school this month?
Number new scholars this month?
What is the average attendance?
Number of pupils for whom tuition is paid?
Number of white pupils?
Number always present?
Number always punctual?
Number over 16 years of age?
Number in alphabet?
Number who spell and read easy lessons?
Number in advanced readers?
Number in geography?
Number in arithmetic?
Number in higher branches?
Number in writing?
Number in needle-work?
Number free before the war?
Have you a Sabbath school?
Have you an industrial school?
State the kind of work done

Location? (town, county, or district.)
Of what grade?
When to close?
What society?
Name of board or committee?
Name of board or committee?
Amount paid for this month?
Amount paid for this month?

Amount paid this month?
Amount paid this month?

How much? —— Colored?
White? —— Female?
Male? ——
Number enrolled last report, by adding new scholars and subtracting those left school, will equal the present total enrolment.

How many teachers? —— How many pupils?
How many teachers? —— How many pupils?

* Or school committee, either district, town, city, county, or State.

† A pupil is not to be reported as enrolled until after five days' attendance.

☞"To the following questions give exact or approximate answers, prefixing to the latter the word "about.""

1. Do you know of any schools for refugees or freedmen not reported to the State superintendent? ———, How many? ———,
2. Give (estimated) whole number of pupils in all such schools. ———, Number of teachers. ———, White ———, Colored ———,
3. Do you know of Sabbath schools not reported to the State superintendent? ———, How many? ———,
4. Give (estimated) whole number of pupils in all such schools. ———, Number of teachers ———, White ———, Colored ———,
5. State the public sentiment towards colored schools. ———
6. How many pupils in your school are members of a temperance society? ———, Name of the society? ———,
Remarks ———

——— ———, *Teacher.*

EXPLANATIONS.

If any of the within questions cannot be answered by the teacher, they may be left for the superintendent. Place each answer, to the extent of your knowledge, opposite the question, and he will fill the remaining spaces.

Night and Sabbath schools taught by a group of teachers should be reported but once.

In the "remarks" notice any important fact which the blank does not call for.

It is hoped that the educational societies will adopt this form of report; if so, the bureau can furnish the blanks.

Should more extended forms be used, it would oblige the Commissioner to have them include all the items of this.

BUREAU OF REFUGEES, FREEDMEN AND ABANDONED LANDS, *Washington, D. C., January* 1, 18—.

[Ed. Form, No. 4.]

Sub-assistant commissioner's (or agent's) monthly report on education of freed-men and refugees in sub-district, State of ————, in charge of ————, for the month of ————. 1868. [in accordance with order contained in circular No. 5, Bureau R., F., & A. L.]

1. Name of your sub-district?
2. Whole number of refugee or freedmen's schools in the district? Day? Night? Sabbath?
3. Location of schools?
4. Whole number of teachers? White? Colored?
5. Names and post office address of day school teachers?
6. Whole number of school-houses for freedmen in your district? Their condition, capacity, value, and by whom owned?
7. Number of your visits to schools? Day? Night? Sabbath?
8. Number of educational meetings held by you during the month? Where?
9. Number and names of places, now destitute, in which day schools might be organized?
10. Number of pupils (estimated) who would attend such schools?
11. Amount which would probably be raised by the freedmen, for school purposes, in each destitute neighborhood?
12. What efforts are you making to secure the support of schools by pupils, parents, boards of education, or the State government?
13. Whole number of additional school-houses, for freedmen, now wanted in your sub-district?
14. Could you organize your sub-districts, each with a school committee pledged to carry on schools therein?
15. To what extent would help from without be needed in such cases?
16. What is the public sentiment as to the education of the freedmen and poor whites?
17. Are night schools for adults needed in your district? In what way could they be carried on?
18. What more can this bureau do for educating the children of refugees (or poor whites?)
19. How long will northern charitable aid be needed for freedmen and refugee schools or your district?

I hereby certify, on honor, that I have given personal attention to the matters herein named, and that the answers given are, according to my best knowledge and belief, correct.

————————————,
Sub-Ass't Com. Bureau R., F., & A. L..